OXFORD SHAKESPEARE STUDIES

*

RE-EDITING SHAKESPEARE
FOR THE MODERN READER

OXFORD SHAKESPEARE STUDIES

Re-Editing Shakespeare for the Modern Reader

BASED ON LECTURES GIVEN AT THE FOLGER SHAKESPEARE LIBRARY, WASHINGTON, DC

STANLEY WELLS

CLARENDON PRESS · OXFORD
1984

Oxford University Press, Walton Street, Oxford OX2 6DP

London New York Toronto
Delhi Bombay Calcutta Madras Karachi
Kuala Lumpur Singapore Hong Kong Tokyo
Nairobi Dar es Salaam Cape Town
Melbourne Auckland

and associated companies in
Beirut Berlin Ibadan Mexico City Nicosia

Oxford is a trade mark of Oxford University Press

Published in the United States
by Oxford University Press, New York

British Library Cataloguing in Publication Data
Wells, Stanley, 1930–
Re-editing Shakespeare for the modern reader.
– (Oxford Shakespeare Studies)
1. Shakespeare, William – Editors
2. Manuscripts – Editing
I. Title
822.3'3   PR3071
ISBN 0-19-812934-3

Typeset by Hope Services, Abingdon.
Printed in Great Britain at
the University Press, Oxford

PREFACE

This little book has its origin in lectures given at the Folger Shakespeare Library, Washington D.C. I am grateful to the Library's Director, Dr O. B. Hardison Jr., to Dr John F. Andrews, Director of its Institute of Renaissance and Eighteenth-Century Studies, and to other members of the Library's staff for help and hospitality.

From an early stage in the life of the Shakespeare department of Oxford University Press, I have worked in the closest collaboration with Gary Taylor, whose rigorous sense of logic and extraordinary command of detail have been a constant stimulus and challenge. While I have endeavoured in the following pages to acknowledge specific suggestions made by him, I am conscious also of a far more pervasive indebtedness.

An Oxford Shakespeare which regrettably did not materialize was to have been edited by R. B. McKerrow. Only his *Prologomena* appeared (Oxford, 1939). As McKerrow says in his Preface, he had hoped that this work 'would be published with the first two volumes (nine plays) of the edition'. Nine plays were in fact set up in type, probably from marked-up facsimiles of early editions for McKerrow to use as working texts. They include some emendations; though we cannot be sure that McKerrow would finally have endorsed them, they are of exceptional interest as evidence of his thinking. The type has been distributed, but proofs were pulled, and I have been fortunate to have access to them. A mass of McKerrow's editorial material, in various states of revision, was in the keeping of Dr Alice Walker until she died in October, 1982: this is now with Oxford University Press. Although it was not available to me until I came to revise my lectures for publication, I have been grateful for the opportunity to consult it.

Quotations from Shakespeare's works are normally given in the spelling and punctuation of the primary editions. Act, scene, and line references are to Peter Alexander's edition (1951); TLN refers to the through line numbering given to each play in *The First Folio of Shakespeare: The Norton Facsimile*, edited by Charlton Hinman (New York, 1968).

I am grateful to Giorgio Melchiori for help with Shakespeare's Italian, to Richard Proudfoot for helpful comments on the typescript, to Christine Avern-Carr for assistance in preparing copy and checking proofs, and to Gary Taylor and John Jowett for assistance with the proofs.

S. W. W.

TABLE OF CONTENTS

INTRODUCTION

The four chapters of this book are a by-product of my experience so far as General Editor of the Oxford Shakespeare. They make no claim to survey the foundations of editorial technique. They are concerned with the presentation as well as with the establishing of Shakespeare's text. The first two look at verbal details of that text, the second two at matters of staging. They address questions such as the justification for modernizing the spelling and punctuation of the early printings of the plays, the need to re-examine traditional emendations, and the propriety and techniques of adding to and altering their original stage directions. These may seem superficial matters, but I hope I show that they deserve more thorough consideration than they have received, and that such consideration may have consequences of no less importance than those resulting from analyses of the work of individual compositors, investigations of the kinds of manuscript underlying the early printed texts, and other bibliographical and textual techniques to which more attention has been paid in recent years. I write, in fact, as an editor rather than as a bibliographer, if this distinction may be allowed. Most studies of editorial theory and practice have come from bibliographical and textual critics who have had very little experience of editing (like W. W. Greg) or whose editing has been largely or entirely confined to old-spelling editions of a more or less diplomatic nature (like R. B. McKerrow and Fredson Bowers). Understandably, such critics have concentrated on the fundamental investigation of textual problems. I, on the other hand, concern myself rather with problems that arise in the process of applying the results of bibliographical studies to the preparation of texts for the modern reader. In the course of doing so, I have been obliged to voice criticisms of other editors. I hope I have done so in a spirit of proper humility. None of us can avoid error; all judgement is both subjective and fallible. Every editor lays himself open to correction of his errors and to criticism of his judgement. But awareness of this should not inhibit him from the exercise of independent judgement.

I hope, too, that what I have to say will demonstrate that to prepare a new edition of Shakespeare is not a waste of time. It is true that many editions of Shakespeare are available to the modern reader.

But it is also true that many people continue to think hard about Shakespeare and, more generally, about various aspects of the times in which he lived. The 1980s have already seen the publication of, for example, a study of Elizabethan theatres (John Orrell's *The Quest for Shakespeare's Globe* (Cambridge, 1983)) which changes our picture of the buildings in which Shakespeare's plays were first performed; a newly discovered document establishing that *Henry VIII* 'had been acted not passing 2 or 3 times before' the Globe burnt down on 29 June 1613 (in Maija Jansson Cole's 'A New Account of the Burning of the Globe', *Shakespeare Quarterly* 32 (1981), p. 352); a thorough reconsideration of Shakespeare's use of proverbs (in R. W. Dent's *Shakespeare's Proverbial Language: An Index* (Berkeley and Los Angeles, 1981)); a rigorous study of pronunciation problems (in Fausto Cercignani's *Shakespeare's Works and Elizabethan Pronunciation* (Oxford, 1982)); the most detailed study ever made of an Elizabethan printing house (in Peter W. M. Blayney's *The Texts of 'King Lear' and their Origins*, Volume I, *Nicholas Okes and the First Quarto* (Cambridge, 1982)); an original examination of the text of *2 Henry IV* (in Eleanor Prosser's *Shakespeare's Anonymous Editors: Scribe and Compositor in the Folio Text of '2 Henry IV'* (Stanford, California, 1981)); several far-reaching studies of the text of *King Lear* (in, most notably, Steven Urkowitz's *Shakespeare's Revision of 'King Lear'* (Princeton, 1980), and *The Division of the Kingdoms*, edited by Gary Taylor and Michael Warren (Oxford, 1983)); and, in various learned journals, a number of studies, some of them building on the work of Charlton Hinman, of the printing of Shakespeare's plays. These and other works have implications for the study of Shakespeare's text, and it is proper that notice should be taken of them in editions of the plays. And, although the editor's most basic task lies in the establishment of a text, editions properly serve many other purposes for a constantly changing readership. They reflect shifts in pedagogical techniques; there is, for instance, far less emphasis on philology in modern editions than there was in editions such as the Pitt Press and the Warwick Shakespeare. There is an increasing emphasis on the plays as texts for performance; there is a readier acceptance, and a freer exposition, of their bawdy elements. New critical thought may be reflected in the Introductions to new editions, and may influence the notes and even the text.

It would, of course, be absurd to suggest that a new edition should be prepared every time someone proposes a new emendation or offers a fresh interpretation of a particular passage. The process is cumulative;

only gradually will a particular edition come to seem out of date. It is not possible in practice to organize events with such delicate precision that a new edition of a particular play appears at the exact moment that an earlier edition of the same play is suddenly seen to be in need of replacement. Nor should we expect every fresh edition of each play to be radically different from its predecessors. It is proper that texts should be freshly examined from time to time in the light of the latest scholarship, but it would be dishonest of an editor to make changes merely so that his edition would be different from someone else's. And of course some editions are in the nature rather of repackagings of existing material in the hope of reaching a market larger than, or different from, that of earlier packagings.

At the time that I accepted the General Editorship of the Oxford Shakespeare, it seemed to me that there was a genuine need for a new edition. The Cambridge edition, edited by John Dover Wilson and others, was acknowledged even by its publishers to be out of date; Cambridge University Press started to plan a fresh edition at about the same time as Oxford. The Arden edition was still in progress, but its earliest volumes, and its general style of presentation, dated from the early 1950s. The New Penguin edition was serving a general readership well, but was not uniformly ambitious in its scholarship; the Pelican and Signet editions were considerably less ambitious, sparser in their annotations, and seemed more American than English in their general orientation. These were the principal competitors in multi-volume editions. So far as complete editions were concerned, there were the Alexander text, admirable in its way, but dating from 1951 (and unattractively printed), the collected Signet and Pelican editions, the rather eccentric Sisson text of 1954, and the Riverside, of 1974, which has a textual policy with which I am not in sympathy, for reasons that I give below.

All these editions are in modern spelling: there was no edition of the complete works in their original spelling and punctuation. I had, then, no misgivings about the propriety of a new edition, and I accept the corollary that my own editorial work will dwindle into obsolescence, forming one thin layer in the coral reef of editorial effort, like that of my predecessors. But I did feel disquiet about a trend in Shakespeare editing which quite understandably leads to charges of redundancy among Shakespeare editions. This is a timorous conservatism which I believe has led many recent editors to an excessive reliance on those texts which seem closest to Shakespeare's original papers rather than to the texts reflecting the theatre practice of his time, and which has also led to a reluctance to emend and to an undue subservience to the editorial tradition. Of course, the desire to conserve is a basic motive in editing; every scholarly editor must be impelled by a respect for the primary evidence. But when he is tempted to ignore considerations suggesting that the primary evidence should be set aside, he should examine himself carefully in an effort to discover whether he is motivated by pure reason or indulging a lazy-minded reluctance to disturb the status quo. I am only too conscious of lethargic impulses within myself, and the effort to identify and counteract them forms a recurrent theme of the pages that follow.

1

OLD AND MODERN SPELLING

It is now over half a century since R. B. McKerrow published the *Prolegomena* for the edition of Shakespeare which he had undertaken for Oxford University Press. This was planned as an old-spelling edition with several plays in each volume. The *Prolegomena* was based on his experience in editing nine or ten plays; but he died not long after it appeared, and the only part of his edition ever to reach publication was the two specimen pages for *Richard III* appended to the *Prolegomena*. At the time I prepared the lectures on which these chapters are based, I had worked, in collaboration with my colleagues, on rather more plays than McKerrow had when he published his *Prolegomena*, and this seemed a good opportunity, and stimulus, to take stock of some of the things that I, in my turn, had learned from the experience. These are not, however, my prolegomena. Partly this is because I am engaged on a far more collaborative project than was McKerrow. The Oxford Shakespeare is a tripartite enterprise. The Oxford English Texts edition, of which the first five volumes have already appeared, will offer new, modern-spelling editions of all the plays, each edited by a different scholar. The *Complete Oxford Shakespeare* will offer independently edited texts of all Shakespeare's works, in one volume. I am working on this with S. Schoenbaum (who will be principally responsible for the Introductions), with Gary Taylor as Associate Editor, with John Jowett as Assistant Editor, and with other colleagues in the Shakespeare department of Oxford University Press. This single-volume edition will be made available in unannotated form, both in modern spelling and in the spelling and punctuation of the original editions, and in a modern-spelling, annotated form. When I became General Editor of the Oxford Shakespeare, I fashioned a substantial set of 'Editorial Procedures' as guide-lines for editors of the Oxford English Texts edition. Nevertheless, I am not entirely happy with the concept of rules for editors. The editing of Shakespeare is a personal business, and it rouses personal passions. No book of rules, however detailed, will compel one editor to edit a play in the same way that someone else—such as his General

Editor—would edit it, however rigorously the rules are worked out, and whatever subtle—or crude—range of persuasive techniques a General Editor may employ in the attempt to enforce them. And another reason that I am not now offering my prolegomena is that such an enterprise seems far less necessary than it was when McKerrow wrote. He was able to say that at the time of beginning work on his edition, in 1929, he had not realized 'how little systematic consideration seemed ever to have been given to editorial methods as applied to English writings in general and those of Shakespeare in particular'. He could point to no more than the preface to the old Cambridge edition, of 1863-6, and Dover Wilson's 'Textual Introduction' to his, later, Cambridge edition, printed along with *The Tempest* in 1921 (*Prolegomena*, p. v).

I need not say that this situation no longer obtains. Editorial methods have been extensively considered, most notably, though by no means exclusively, by W. W. Greg and Fredson Bowers. New editorial theories have been propounded, new techniques have been devised, and new tools have appeared, some in the form of reference works, some technological. Properly trained editors know how to go about their business. Nevertheless, a good many options are open to them. McKerrow states in his opening sentence that there might be 'at least half a dozen editions of the works of Shakespeare executed on quite different lines, each of which, to one group of readers, would be the best edition possible'. It is up to a General Editor to indicate which of the options should be followed, which are the 'lines' on which this particular edition should be executed; he also has the opportunity to provide guide-lines particularly for any areas of the work which, he feels, have not been adequately covered in scholarly studies already published. It is with some of these matters as they have presented themselves to me in the course of my work that I shall concern myself in these chapters.

Discussing the options open to him, McKerrow mentions as one extreme a text 'completely modernized both in spelling and punctuation, with full stage directions', and as the other extreme, 'a photographic reproduction of the early prints or, failing this, a facsimile reprint'. Between the extremes come the kinds of edition on which he is engaged: those which 'attempt to present Shakespeare's work as nearly in the form in which he left it as the evidence which we have permits, clearing it indeed as far as possible of the numerous errors with which the ignorance and carelessness of copyists and printers have disfigured it, but without superfluous comment or any attempt to improve upon the text as the author left it'. His edition will be 'among the more conservative' of these.[1]

There were good reasons why McKerrow should prefer to produce an old-spelling edition. He had thus edited the works of Thomas Nashe, in what remains one of the most impressive of all editions of an English author. He was commissioned by a press which had a policy of publishing editions for the scholar (Oxford English Texts) and then of reworking them, with modernized spelling and other changes, for the general reader (Oxford Standard Authors), and which also produced school editions (for example the Clarendon Shakespeare) which too could derive from a parent text. No doubt McKerrow found it easier to concentrate upon the problems of the text if he was not required to add the problems of modernizing to his other anxieties. He does not, so far as I can see, appear to have had any strong feelings about the relative merits of old and modern spelling, but other scholars have had such feelings—with some of them, indeed, it has come to seem a moral rather than an intellectual issue. Hackles are raised by it. Once, for example, I telephoned a professor of English language to ask for advice on the modernization of a specific word. He reacted as if I had made an improper suggestion. All he could think of to say in favour of modernized texts was that they might at least help a few people to read Shakespeare who would otherwise be reading Agatha Christie. Too late, after I had put the receiver down, I thought of asking him in what editions *he* read Shakespeare, since no remotely satisfactory old-spelling edition exists. Although a few authors of critical and other works on Shakespeare quote from an early edition, my experience is that while students of the language may prefer old-spelling editions for working purposes, those concerned with literary and dramatic values are happy with modernized versions. Even Philip Gaskell, who disapproves of modernization in general, admits (in his book *From Writer to Reader*) that 'we have all read Shakespeare . . . in modernized texts without coming to much harm'.[2] But this is a grudging consolation, and I think it may be worth looking at the arguments once again to see if any more positive considerations emerge.

Gaskell makes a succinct statement of the objections to modernizing: 'The deliberate modernization of the spelling, punctuation, etc. of an early text is undesirable because it suggests that the modern meaning

---

[1] *Prolegomena* (Oxford, 1939), pp. 1–2.
[2] *From Writer to Reader* (Oxford, 1978), p. 8.

of the words of the text is what the author meant by them; because it conceals puns and rhymes; because it causes the editor to choose where the author was ambiguous; and because it deprives the work of the quality of belonging to its own period.'[3] Gaskell goes on to admit that 'even the most scrupulous editor may be obliged to modernize' texts of the sixteenth and seventeenth centuries for the benefit of non-specialist readers; then 'the editor must be prepared to modernize, however much he dislikes it'. This evokes a pitiable vision of an editor gritting his teeth and nobly forcing himself to knock off final 'e's and otherwise mutilate words against all his more humane (or human) instincts. Let us examine the objections in more detail.

First, 'modernization . . . suggests that the modern meaning of the words . . . is what the author meant by them'. This is a rather vague objection. The spelling of many words was the same in Shakespeare's time as it is now, though their meaning may have shifted either subtly or, in some cases, drastically. An old-spelling text will do nothing to alert the reader to their earlier significations. For some words, the old spelling may act as a complete disguise, concealing any meaning from an untrained modern reader. Admittedly this may cause him to look the word up, but he may then discover nothing different in the Elizabethan from the modern sense (as, for example, if he had been confused by the spelling 'serieant' for 'sergeant', at *Comedy of Errors*, 4.2.56, TLN 1168, etc.), and in the mean time his reading experience will have been interrupted. A reader would be more efficiently reminded of the need for *constant* vigilance about meaning if the text were printed on yellowing paper or in an old-fashioned type. Anyone conscientious enough to overcome the deterrents of unfamiliar spelling and to let its presence in some words act as a stimulant to lexical investigation of *all* words in a text might be alert enough to remember even in a modern-spelling version that he is reading a work by Shakespeare; and even without old spelling, quite a lot would remain to act as a frequent reminder of this fact. So, although I see a certain force in this objection, I would not accord it much weight.

---

[3] Although Gaskell admits later in his book that 'Plays are different . . .' (see pp. 12–13 below), he reiterated the same objections, in different terms, in his review (*Cambridge Review*, 2 May 1980, 158–9) of my *Modernizing Shakespeare's Spelling*, so it seems fair to cite them here. An interesting discussion of the propriety and technique of modernizing a non-dramatic text is to be found in 'Editorial Problems in Milton. Part I' by John Creaser, in *Review of English Studies* 34 (1983), 279–303.

Gaskell's second objection is that modernizing 'conceals puns and rhymes'; his third is that it 'causes the editor to choose when the author was ambiguous'. I take these two together because so far as I can see the only way in which modernizing can conceal a pun is when it destroys ambiguity, though the destruction of ambiguity is not necessarily identical with the suppression of a pun. Arthur Brown provided examples (cited by Bowers[4]) in *A Midsummer Night's Dream* of the destruction of ambiguity necessitated by the modern use of the apostrophe, in 'light them at the fiery Glowe-wormes eyes' (3.1.156) and in the word 'fortunes' in Lysander's lines

> I am my Lord, as well deriu'd as hee,
> As well possest; my loue is more than his:
> My fortunes euery way as fairely rankt . . .
>   (Q1, 1600; 1.1.99–101)

It is true that correct use of the apostrophe destroys ambiguity in such lines, and true, too, that in these lines, no one can be certain whether Shakespeare wished to refer to one or more glow-worms, or to use 'fortunes' as a plural noun, or as a singular noun followed by an ellipsis of 'is'. If, however, we are experiencing the plays in the theatre—for which, as we all know, they were written—the editor's agonies are rendered redundant and the ambiguity, unimpeded by the constraints of typography, may work effortlessly upon our receptive consciousness.

Bowers points also to uncertainties caused by the fact that Elizabethan spelling sometimes makes no distinction between meanings now kept apart by distinct spellings. He instances 'the Elizabethan doublet *travel–travail*', pointing out that, while 'Sometimes Shakespeare keeps the precise meanings of the two absolutely distinct', at other times 'he seems to intend both meanings simultaneously, a device aided by the fact that "travel" was often spelled "travail" anyway'. In such situations, Bowers claims, a modernizing editor who obscures 'the possible evidence by modernizing all *travail* forms to *travel* whenever the sense permits . . . changes Shakespeare's probable intentions in an unwarranted manner and detracts from the vitality of the language and the subtle meaning that Shakespeare may have intended'. He gives some examples 'in which, in the original editions, the spelling is *travail*, with what seems . . . to be the strong possibility of a pun, but the Globe text silently changes to *travel* and is conscientiously followed by

---

[4] *On Editing Shakespeare* (Charlottesville, Virginia, 1966), pp. 157–8.

Kittredge and Alexander' (pp. 158-9). Bowers is undoubtedly right, but at the same time it might be objected that for the modern reader, at least, the Elizabethan spelling also obscures one side of the pun–or, for that matter, that it suggests a pun where none was intended. I believe myself that a modernizing editor should select what he regards as the primary meaning, irrespective of the original spelling, print this, and annotate the secondary meaning. It is not always easy to decide on the primary meaning–as usual, the old-spelling editor has the simpler task; but I fail to see how *any* editor can convey the double meaning; the only advantage of the old spelling is that, to a knowledgeable reader, it is more open of meaning than the modern spelling, though the openness will be evident only to a trained eye (which would be alert to it even in a modern-spelling edition).

Bowers also gives two examples of punctuation in which the adoption of a modern system requires the kind of choice which may, he says, 'support one meaning over another, or support one idiomatic usage against its contrary'. This may sometimes happen; if so, the examples that Bowers gives are not well chosen. The first, from *Hamlet*, is Marcellus's

> Therefore I haue intreated him along,
> With vs to watch the minuts of this night . . .
>   (Q2; 1.1.26–7)

where F1 has the comma after 'vs', not after 'along'. Bowers complains that editors who omit all punctuation 'leave the matter ambiguously open to the reader's conjecture–to the loss of Shakespeare's probable intention' (p. 162), but this is a complaint against one particular modernization, not against the process itself; as Bowers says, approvingly, Kittredge follows Q2 in a modernized text. Bowers's other example is the very different punctuation in Q2 and in F of Hamlet's 'What peece of worke is a man . . .' (2.2.305 ff.); Bowers complains that in a modernized text the reader cannot tell that 'there may be two sides to this moving speech' (p. 163), but exactly the same is true in an old-spelling text. Nor does Bowers mention the innumerable points in the original texts at which the punctuation, though unexceptionable in its own terms, is misleading not only to a non-specialist modern reader but even to a linguist, at least until he has reread the passage to work out its sense. There are, for example, places where a comma is used where we should use a hyphen, as between 'marriage' and 'blessing' in

Iu⟨no⟩. Honor, riches, marriage, blessing . . .
(*Tempest* 4.1.106, TLN 1767)

Parentheses are often oddly used, yet in ways which, however illogical they may seem to us, appear to have been acceptable at the time the texts were printed. In Sonnet 86, for instance, they serve a function that hyphens would serve in modern punctuation:

> Was it the proud full saile of his great verse,
> Bound for the prize of (all to precious) you . . .

I should hesitate to alter this in an old-spelling edition; but it is un-doubtedly liable to mislead. What McKerrow wrote in 1939 is no less true today: 'the subject of punctuation is one which bristles with difficulties, and there is still much work to be done before it will be possible to say what usages would have been regarded, by an educated Elizabethan, as allowable and what would have been regarded as definitely wrong' (*Prolegomena*, p. 41).

In short, it seems to me that as the whole point of an old-spelling edition is to preserve unfamiliar usages it should be highly conservative in its treatment of the accidentals of the text, and that any such edition must preserve features which will obscure meaning to a far greater degree than the partially interpretative decisions forced upon a modernizing editor. I am not presenting this point as an absolute denial of the value of an old-spelling edition; I am objecting to a statement of a limitation of the modernizing process which neglects to admit the correspondingly limited expressiveness of aspects of the original text.

G. Blakemore Evans has provided additional examples of problems arising from 'the use of a common single spelling form for words of different meaning': thus, 'loose' and 'lose', 'humane' and 'human', 'I' and 'Ay', 'then' and 'than', 'born' and 'borne', 'lest' and 'least', 'of' and 'off' are, as he says, all confusible; so are 'cheerly' and 'cheerily', and we may be uncertain whether 'farre' means 'far' or 'farther'. When ambiguity is possible, I quite agree with Evans that 'an editor owes it to his reader to admit the presence of such ambiguity in a textual or glossarial note'.[5] This procedure is applicable equally in annotated old- or modern-spelling editions.

Gaskell also refers to the concealment of rhymes as a result of the modernizing process, and it is undeniable that total modernization

---

[5] *'Shakespeare Restored* – Once Again!', in *Editing Renaissance Dramatic Texts*, ed. Anne Lancashire (New York and London, 1976), pp. 39–56; pp. 48, 49.

would have this effect in some cases. Again, however, it is only fair to recall that early spelling itself does not always accord with a rhyme. In *Love's Labour's Lost*, for example, 'carue' rhymes with 'serue' (Q1; 4.1.55-6); in *King Lear* we have the rhymes 'caught her', 'daughter', 'slaughter', 'halter', and 'after' (Q1; 1.4.318-22); in *Henry V*, 'Charge' rhymes with *'George'* (F1; 3.1.33-4); in *Venus and Adonis*, 'chat' with 'gate' (Q1; 422, 424); in *Romeo and Juliet*, 'Nurse' with 'course' (meaning 'corpse'; Q2; 3.2.127-8). These are just a few of the many points at which an old-spelling reading does not provide an eye-rhyme. It is true that the editor who modernizes 'course' to 'corpse' will not suggest much of a rhyme with 'nurse'; but neither does the editor who retains 'course'. Still, I do not deny that a fully modernized text would obscure rhyme, and that an editor of Sonnet 34, coming upon the couplet

> Ah but those teares are pearle which thy loue sheeds,
> And they are ritch, and ransome all ill deeds

would be understandably torn between retaining 'sheeds' at the expense of sense and modernizing to 'sheds' while obscuring the rhyme.

Gaskell's fourth objection is that modernizing 'deprives the work of the quality of belonging to its own period'. Again, I find this vague. Modern paper, modern typography, modern binding all have the same effect; so even does the ageing process on early copies. Gaskell presumably feels that there is no justification for wantonly adding to inevitable distancing factors, but the point of view is at least tenable that we place ourselves at a greater distance from a literary work by retaining the accidentals of its original presentation than by sweeping them away. As John Russell Brown has written, '"Old-Spelling" was neither old nor odd nor distinctive' to Elizabethan authors and readers, 'and it is impossible for us to read a play as they did. The "Elizabethan flavour" of an old-spelling text is a modern phenomenon.' From this, he concludes that 'its dissemination can do no service to the original authors or their works'.[6]

That may be pitching it a bit high; what is indisputable is that, as Gaskell admits (though he does not follow it up in relation to sixteenth- or seventeenth-century texts), 'Plays are different from the works of literature that we have been considering so far because they are

---

[6] 'The Rationale of Old-Spelling Editions of the Plays of Shakespeare and his Contemporaries', *Studies in Bibliography* 13 (1960), 49–67; p. 61.

completed and primarily communicated not as books to be read but as performances in the theatre' (p. 9). Although attempts have been made to act plays by Shakespeare in Elizabethan pronunciation, there is no way in which they could be acted in Elizabethan spelling, punctuation, and capitalization—though the story goes that when Charles Laughton was rehearsing Lear at Stratford-upon-Avon he got his wife to sit in the stalls with a facsimile of the Folio and the instruction to shout out whenever he was due to speak a word printed with a capital letter, so that he could duly stress it. The very effort to imagine such an absurdity should alert us to one of the major disadvantages of an old-spelling edition: that it creates too many distractions from the aesthetic experience, 'refrigerating the mind' (in Dr Johnson's phrase) with interruption and irrelevancy.

In considering the objections to modernization set forth by Gaskell, Bowers, and others, I have conceded that a modernizing editor may sometimes have to make decisions which limit the range of meaning discernible in the original form of the text, and that he may sometimes have difficulty with rhymes. He is likely too to increase the precision of the punctuation, and in the process may sometimes make questionable decisions. I do not deny that these objections deserve to be considered. I realize, too, that some people read early texts not always for the literary (or quasi-dramatic) experience they may afford, but rather in the pursuit of other, legitimate, scholarly ends. Bowers puts the point:

A reader of a dramatic text in search of information about Elizabethan idiom, usage, possible and impossible spelling forms, morphological variants, ... metrics, the author's use of hypermetrical lines, short lines, caesural pause, feminine endings, rhyme, syncopation of syllables ... is as much a critical user of the edition as the one who is concerned with the philosophical import of the theme of reconciliation in Shakespeare's last plays.[7]

Let us grant that some of the categories of reader posited here need to be able to read Shakespeare's plays in the spelling and punctuation of the original editions, and that photographic facsimiles are inadequate for their purposes. They need an edited text, and one of our plans is to provide them with one. But let us not pretend that an old-spelling edition does not have serious disadvantages. I return again to McKerrow: 'there might ... be at least half a dozen editions of the works of Shakespeare executed on quite different lines, each of which, to one

---

[7] *Textual and Literary Criticism* (Cambridge, 1959; repr. 1966), pp. 143-4.

group of readers, would be the best edition possible.' There is no moral superiority in belonging to the class of readers best served by an old-spelling edition.

Perhaps the least logical claim for the superiority of such an edition was made by Fredson Bowers. Asking 'Wherein is an old-spelling edition more authoritative in its form than a modernized text?', he replies 'For one thing, an old-spelling edition must refer directly back to the originals, whereas every modernized text is formed by annotation of the pasted-up pages of some preceding editor's version, and is likely, as a consequence, to repeat, inadvertently, some of its errors that were not detected. A long history of the careless transmission of error by this means can be written.'[8] That this practice has prevailed is undeniable. McKerrow had deplored it in similar terms: 'the general practice of the earlier editors, with the exception of Capell, and of many of their modern successors, of working upon a recent edition in order to prepare their own, revising this when, and only when, it seemed to them in error, has tended to obscure the practices of the early texts and to give permanence to innumerable departures from them in points of detail' (*Prolegomena*, p. 3). It is, regrettably, true that, so far as I can discover, every one-volume edition of the complete works— even the First Folio itself—has been made up in this fashion except for collective editions such as the Pelican and Signet, whose individual editors may or may not have worked in this way. Editors in multi-volume series may have used the same method. It is a bad procedure, not merely because it may result in the perpetuation of actual error, but because it inhibits thorough reconsideration of all details of the text, producing editions which are virtual palimpsests.[9] But it is not a necessary procedure, nor is it a universal one. Bowers's statement 'an old-spelling edition is likely to be a work of scholarship' (*On Editing Shakespeare*, pp. 155–6), with the implication that it differs in this respect from a modern-spelling edition, is an unfair aspersion on modernized editions. One has only to look at the editions of A. B. Grosart to see that an old-spelling editor can (or could) get away with murder. (There is a disarming admission of this in Grosart's edition of *Selimus*, published by Dent in 1898. Referring to his old-spelling

---

[8] *On Editing Shakespeare*, p. 155.

[9] Cf. Bowers: 'It is very much an anachronism that so many of our present-day modernised texts retain the heavy eighteenth-century style of pointing because of the indolence of editors unwilling to take the trouble to alter the pointing of the out-of-date edition they have chosen to send to the printer' (*Textual and Literary Criticism*, p. 139).

edition of Greene's works which preceded this, Grosart writes: 'By one of those vexatious accidents to which the best copyists are liable, my copyist turned over the wrong page, and so left out ll. 100–171, and ll. 644–5. Both are important restorations, and I suggest, with sincere apology, their being written in in the play in vol. xiv of the Works.')

I can state as a fact that every volume of the New Penguin Shakespeare has been printed from the editor's typescript, not from a paste-up of an earlier edition. I cannot state as a fact that no editor in that series typed his text (or had it typed) from an earlier edited version: but certainly I have never edited a play in this way, but have always typed my own texts direct from a quarto or Folio facsimile. And this is the way work began on the *Complete Oxford Shakespeare*. But after two or three texts had been edited like this we made a discovery of some practical importance. Trevor Howard-Hill prepared a series of Oxford Concordances to individual plays by Shakespeare, each based on the copy-text selected by Dr Alice Walker for her planned edition. These concordances were printed from computer tapes on to which the original texts had been typed, and which had been proof-read with great care. Learning that these tapes were still in the possession of the Press (which had financed their production), I realized that it would be an economy of effort to abandon my amateurish typing and to work directly on to print-outs made from the tapes. Some modifications have had to be made, especially, of course, in plays existing in collateral texts. We have had to add the deposition scene from the Folio to the First Quarto of *Richard II*, the 'fly' scene to the First Quarto of *Titus Andronicus*, and so on. We check every text again for ourselves (with increasing admiration for Howard-Hill's standards of accuracy); we reconsider Howard-Hill's emendations of accidentals (occasionally he has 'corrected' legitimate contemporary spellings); we work always with photographic facsimiles beside us, and normally check them against original editions. But the method saves us, not just a lot of typing, but also a lot of checking of typescripts and proof-correction of printed texts.

No less importantly, the existence of the tapes gives us a unique opportunity to provide, at what we hope will not be an inordinate cost, a complete edition of Shakespeare's works in their original spelling and punctuation. We should not have contemplated this without the tapes, because the task of ensuring accuracy of reproduction would have been too time-consuming and so too expensive. But a proportion of the work had already been done, and Professor

Hans Walter Gabler, of the University of Munich, has supplied a computer program which greatly facilitates the checking of the edited old-spelling texts against the original transcriptions. So we are doing in fact what all editors of modern-spelling texts do, up to a point, in theory— that is, prepare an old-spelling text as a preliminary stage to preparing one in modern dress. We have, of course, had to make many decisions about points of detail which I shall not go into here. In accidentals, the edition will be highly conservative, because, as I have indicated, I think that those who may use such a text are likely to want it as pure as possible. But it will also be fully edited: the directions will be very close to those of the modern-spelling edition, and it will include all the emendations of that edition. Gary Taylor has collaborated with Mr Lou Burnard, of the Oxford University Computing Service, in the preparation of compositor indexes to the Folio; this means that, for all the plays with Folio copy-texts, we can use the appropriate compositor's preferred spelling (where known) in emendations and added directions. The same process can be applied to the quartos. The edition will have its own through line numbering, and so will, for the first time, enable scholars to quote from, and refer to, the complete works of Shakespeare in edited form but in the spelling and punctuation of their most authoritative early appearance in print.

While I am pleased to think that, if all goes well, we shall in this way fill a major gap in works of Shakespeare scholarship, I have felt from the start of the enterprise that the Oxford English Texts Shakespeare, as well as the new *Complete Oxford Shakespeare*, should be in modern spelling. Admittedly, one among the six types of edition that McKerrow was able to envisage and which I could endorse might well be one that presented the texts in old spelling and accompanied them with a detailed commentary on the language prepared with considerably more thoroughness than that which McKerrow appears, on the evidence of his two pages from *Richard III* as well as his statements in the *Prolegomena* (pp. 100–1), to have proposed to himself. But such an enterprise is rendered partially redundant by the resuscitated New Variorum edition, and, although it would have its value, it would not be conspicuously useful to the great variety of readers, let alone to directors and actors. I believed also, and I believe even more strongly now, that the preparation of modern-spelling editions is likely to result in a fuller exploration of the text, and so in a more thorough work of scholarship, than the preparation of an old-spelling edition, provided that the editor is genuinely concerned to rethink the modernizing process, not merely to follow unthinkingly in the footsteps of his precursors. This is an area which has remained largely uninvestigated since McKerrow's time, mainly, perhaps, because the principal writers on editorial theory have been concerned rather with old-spelling editions.

Greg, who appears to have been completely opposed to modernization, writes entirely in terms of old-spelling texts. Bowers comments that modernized editions 'have their special problems about which much could be said, and indeed at least one such editor believes that the problem of consistent practice in a modernized text is more acute than in old-spelling. It would surely be useful if an experienced editor could set down a reasoned account of the special difficulties in these texts, and his proposed solutions. Fortunately, for me this is outside the scope of enquiry' (for the lectures on which he was engaged).[10] In a footnote to a later lecture, he again remarks that 'editors engaged in modernisations of texts would be well advised to discuss their difficulties more fully in print for their mutual advantage and the formulation of some working conventions that will do the least damage. The guidance that single editors of recent Elizabethan series have received from general editorial instructions both in England and in America has certainly been insufficient.'[11] In the fifteen or so years before I took up my appointment at Oxford I had been strongly aware of this, particularly perhaps because the first author whose works I edited in modernized texts was Thomas Nashe. As most of the works I was including had not previously been modernized I could not have marked up paste-ups of previous editions, even had I wanted to do so; and Nashe's language is so eccentric that it constantly requires difficult decisions. For these reasons it seemed to me necessary to make a serious investigation of the problems of modernizing in the hope of providing both a foundation for the *Complete Oxford Shakespeare* and a more adequate set of general editorial recommendations to those embarking on editions for the Oxford English Texts Shakespeare than had been previously attempted. I published my findings in an essay called 'Modernizing Shakespeare's Spelling',[12] which I do not intend to repeat here; but I should like to say a little about some of the thinking that lay behind it, and about some of its practical consequences.

[10] *On Editing Shakespeare*, p. 69.
[11] *Textual and Literary Criticism*, p. 180.
[12] Stanley Wells and Gary Taylor, *Modernizing Shakespeare's Spelling, with Three Studies in the Text of* Henry V (Oxford, 1979).

Until, so far as I can tell, about the middle of the present century Shakespeare editors were content to follow the policy stated by W. J. Craig in the Preface (1894) to his Oxford edition of the Complete Works: 'For the uncertain orthography of the old editions I have substituted the recognized orthography of the present day. But metrical considerations occasionally render the retention of the older spelling necessary, and I have deemed it desirable to adhere to the older forms of a few words which modern orthography has practically shaped anew.' Dover Wilson, some thirty years later, remarked, 'the spelling of the old texts has been modernised, save for a few Shakespearian forms which seemed worth preserving either for the sake of their quaintness or because the original gives help to the meaning, ease to the scansion or grace to a rhyme'. Otherwise he dismisses the case for old spelling, 'for the simple reason that the spelling of the Folio and Quartos is normally not that of Shakespeare'.[13] Peter Alexander says nothing in his edition on the subject, Kittredge and Sisson simply say that the spelling has been modernized. Possibly the stimulant for the concern that eventually showed itself came from the 'Note on Accidental Characteristics of the Text' which Greg appended to his 'Prolegomena' in *The Editorial Problem in Shakespeare*, first published in 1942 and reprinted in 1951. He claims there that, 'Whatever practice may be thought desirable in a popular or reading edition, in a critical—that is, a critics'—edition modern opinion is unanimously in favour of preserving the spelling and punctuation of the original authority . . .experience has amply proved' that 'modernization on the lines usually followed does quite seriously misrepresent Elizabethan English . . . To print *banquet* for *banket*, *fathom* for *faddom*, *lantern* for *lanthorn*, *murder* for *murther*, *mushroom* for *mushrump*, *orphan* for *orphant*, *perfect* for *parfit*, *portcullis* for *perculace*, *tattered* for *tottered*, *vile* for *vild*, *wreck* for *wrack*, and so on, and so on, is sheer perversion.'[14]

Greg's reference to 'a critical—that is, a critics'—edition' is tendentious. Presumably he is thinking rather of textual than of literary (or dramatic) critics; it is then remarkable that he defies his own principles to the extent of giving all his quotations in modern spelling: even the justification (p. i) that 'in preparing lectures for oral delivery there could be no point in retaining the original spelling in quotations' is somewhat vitiated by the fact that his main objection to modern spelling is that

[13] *The Tempest*, ed. Sir Arthur Quiller-Couch and John Dover Wilson (Cambridge, 1921; repr. 1948), p. xxxix.
[14] Oxford, 1951, pp. l-li.

it destroys traces of Shakespeare's pronunciation. Anyhow, he seems to have aroused anxiety symptoms in editors with aspirations to produce something more important than 'a popular or reading edition'; in particular, a number of the early new Arden editors restored the spellings that Greg mentions, along with others. The Arden series is not notable for consistency of procedure from one volume to another—indeed, its adaptability to changes in thought has been one of its strengths—but J. C. Maxwell, in his 1953 edition of *Titus Andronicus*, says that it is 'In accordance with the principles of this series' that he has 'retained all older forms that are more than variant spellings: hence the reader will find "murther", "banket" and "cur'sy"' (pp. xx-xxi). He does not attempt to define the distinction between the 'form' and the 'spelling' of a word, which in my experience is often difficult to maintain.

The most extreme exponent of compromise is G. Blakemore Evans in his Riverside edition (Boston, Mass., 1974), which seems to me to take the process to its *reductio ad absurdum* in its declared attempt 'to preserve a selection of Elizabethan spelling forms that reflect, or may reflect, a distinctive contemporary pronunciation, both those that are invariant in the early printed texts and those that appear beside the spellings familiar today and so suggest possible variant pronunciations of single words' (p. 39). I have elsewhere stated some of my objections to this policy,[15] and will reiterate here only my conviction that it rests upon the fallacious assumption of a far greater degree of correlation between spelling and pronunciation in both Elizabethan and modern English than is justified by the evidence. If Elizabethan spelling had been genuinely phonetic, there would have been no stimulus to the many contemporary advocates of spelling reform whose works are described in the first volume of E. J. Dobson's classic study, *English Pronunciation 1500-1700* (2 vols., Oxford, 1968). Undoubtedly, in some cases, some Elizabethan spellings give a modern reader a more accurate impression of the pronunciations likely to have been used in Shakespeare's time than would the modern, standardized spelling of these words. But spelling provides only one kind of evidence in phoneticians' attempts to reconstruct Elizabethan pronunciation, and it is a kind that needs to be interpreted by experts. A glance at Fausto Cercignani's *Elizabethan Pronunciation and Shakespeare's Works* (Oxford, 1981) should disabuse anyone of the

---

[15] *Modernizing Shakespeare's Spelling*, pp. 4–5.

illusion that spelling provides anything other than the most partial guide to some aspects of the pronunciation of the period. Shakespeare himself satirizes this notion when he causes Holofernes to condemn Armado as a 'racker of orthagraphie' because he would say 'det, when he shold pronounce debt; d e b t, not det: he clepeth a Calfe, Caufe: halfe, haufe: neighbour *vocatur* nebour; neigh abreuiated ne: this is abhominable, which he would call abbominable . . .' (5.1.20 ff.).

Furthermore, it seems to me quite absurd to retain (or, in some cases, normalize) old spellings which are phonetically close to the modern pronunciation of the word merely because the modern spelling of the same word would be pronounced differently if modern spelling were phonetic. On a number of occasions the Riverside prints 'We'nsday', as if anyone in his senses—even an American who thinks that 'Warwick' rhymes with 'four-wick', or an Englishman who thinks that 'Arkansas' rhymes with 'Kansas'—would ever be in danger of saying 'Wed-nes-day'. The Riverside policy forces it into such manifest absurdities as spelling against the rhyme:

> That made great Jove to humble him to her hand,
> When with his knees he kiss'd the Cretan strond.
> (*The Taming of the Shrew* 1.1.164–5)

This example alone is surely enough to illustrate the fallacy of relying on spelling as a guide to pronunciation. In *Love's Labour's Lost*, the editor retains the spelling 'person' (for 'parson'), even though it is well known that the '-er' spelling often represents the modern 'ar', as in Shakespeare's rhymes 'art-convert', 'desert-impart', and so on, and although the retention necessitates the gloss '*person* parson'. In most ways, the Riverside text is more worthy of respect than that of any twentieth-century edition of the collected works except those of Kittredge and Alexander; I have described it as 'the ideal desert-island Shakespeare';[16] but I thought that its attitude towards modernization was a severely retrograde step years before I ever thought that I should supervise a collected edition myself, and I think so still.

Certainly sound is important in verse, but we should not deceive ourselves into the belief that we will help readers to hear the music of Shakespeare's words with any degree of authenticity merely by retaining 'a selection of Elizabethan spelling forms that reflects, or may reflect, a distinctive contemporary pronunciation . . .'. The point was

---

[16] *Shakespeare: the Writer and his Work* (London, 1978), p. 82.

made by John Russell Brown as one of his reactions to the passage that I have quoted (p. 18) from Greg: 'It is hardly relevant to bring up the question of pronunciation in this connection, for if it would be hard to make a consistent attempt to speak the speeches from an autograph manuscript as the author would have pronounced them, it would be impossible to pronounce them in any meaningful fashion from the doubly or trebly confused orthography of a printed book. And failing a consistent Elizabethan pronunciation, there seems little point in restoring a partial "Elizabethan" pronunciation to those few words whose old spellings more clearly suggest a sound different from the customary modern ones.'[17] Anyone who really believes that a selection from the spectrum of pronunciations available to Elizabethans is essential to the appreciation of Shakespeare needs a phonetic reconstruction (and would have to learn to read it). Otherwise, he must make do either with the imperfect signals of an old-spelling edition, or with the overall commitment to sense that is the only logical course for a modern-spelling edition. Of course, there are exceptions; it may be desirable to retain old spelling in verse when it suggests a syllabification different from that of the modern spelling and necessary for the verse rhythm; and it is sometimes necessary for the communication of rhyme, word-play, and characterful idiosyncrasy. In my essay on modernizing, I wrote that 'to retain some early spellings simply because the editor regards them as aurally preferable is like playing occasional notes of a Beethoven sonata on a fortepiano while the rest are played on a modern grand piano; it adds phonetic confusion to orthographical inconsistency' (pp. 7-8). I would add only that there is an important difference between the world of music and that of the spoken word. Old instruments survive; old speakers do not.

Perhaps because it usually takes longer to edit the complete works than to edit a single play, by the time the Riverside edition appeared the Arden edition had largely abandoned its policy of retention of old spellings for phonetic reasons. The practice had encountered strong resistance. In 1955, Alice Walker wrote that the only alternative to old spelling was 'full modernization'[18] and she argued the case against partial modernization more fully in an article published in the following year.[19] In the same year Arthur Brown—who became General Editor

[17] 'The Rationale of Old-Spelling Editions', p. 61.
[18] 'Compositor Determination and Other Problems in Shakespearian Texts', *Studies in Bibliography* 7 (1955), 3-15; p. 9.
[19] 'Some Editorial Principles (with Special Reference to *Henry V*)', *Studies in Bibliography* 8 (1956), 95-111; see especially pp. 109-10.

of the Malone Society, which prints type-facsimiles of old plays, and who is usually thought of as a proponent of old spelling—wrote in a discussion of what he called 'Semi-Popular Editions', 'For the present writer, at least, complete modernisation as far as this is attainable has seemed to be the right principle'; he also acknowledged that 'The way of the modernised spelling editor is hard compared with that of his old spelling colleague; the points mentioned so far may be small ones, but they occur frequently and require a decision each time, and the cumulative effect is wearying!'[20] (Perhaps this is why, although Arthur Brown contracted to edit *Much Ado About Nothing* and *A Midsummer Night's Dream* for the Arden edition, he abandoned both: Fredson Bowers's praise for the Arden edition of *Much Ado*, which in a book published in 1966 he declared to 'have been edited with scrupulous care for the bibliographical history of the text',[21] anticipated the publication of that volume by sixteen years, during which it went through two different changes of announced editorship.)

A year or so later, Fredson Bowers was attacking 'partial modernisation' as producing 'A fake Elizabethan English', and was asserting that his own sympathies lay with 'complete and absolute modernisation'.[22] General practice in paperback editions such as the Signet, Pelican, and New Penguin favoured 'complete' modernization, though individual editors within the various series fluctuate in their practice. I suppose that such editions count as 'popular' or at best 'semi-popular', rather than 'scholarly' or 'critical', though, for example, Pelican editors include scholars such as Fredson Bowers, R. C. Bald, Matthew Black, and George Walton Williams who have worked on old-spelling editions and who should not be lightly suspected of lowering their standards in going over to modern spelling. It is necessary to insist that the fact that full modernization makes texts more intelligible to a wide readership than partial or non-modernization must not be taken to mean that modernization may not be undertaken in the purest spirit of scholarship, or that a modernized edition is by its nature inferior to an old-spelling edition. The practice of modern-spelling editors has often left something to be desired, but to say this is not to criticize the policy. A notable step forward was the publication in 1970 of Jürgen Schäfer's article 'The Orthography of Proper Names in Modern-spelling

---

[20] 'Editorial Problems in Shakespeare: Semi-Popular Editions', *Studies in Bibliography* 8 (1956), 15–26; pp. 19–20.

[21] *On Editing Shakespeare*, p. 152.

[22] *Textual and Literary Criticism*, pp. 133 ff.

Editions of Shakespeare',[23] in which the author remarks that the 'historical and significant names' have never been 'consistently subjected to the principle of modernization nor to any other editorial principle'. Schäfer finds that, up to the time of the (old) Cambridge edition, 'editors had been following a general policy of gradually modernizing one historical name after another', though they had not done so with any thoroughness: the Cambridge editors 'seem to have frozen the text at the stage they encountered; they neither returned to the old forms nor did they add any modernized ones'. But 'a few decades later the movement of the preceding centuries towards modernization is reversed', first, early in the twentieth century, by the abandonment of modernized forms affecting the metre, second, starting with Kittredge (1936), by the return to spellings (such as 'Frankford' and 'Harflew') suggestive of Elizabethan pronunciation 'although the prosody as such is not affected'. Schäfer defines various objections to 'this new editorial attitude': that 'the uniformity of names occurring in variant forms is put in jeopardy'; 'that many of the resulting forms are meaningless to the modern reader without an explanatory footnote'; that it is questionable 'whether place-names in their Elizabethan form are compatible with a text that is in other regards fully modernized'; that, if pronunciation is to be a criterion, the argument 'fails to take into account place-names [such as "Rome"] whose Elizabethan orthography coincides with the modern but whose Elizabethan pronunciation was considerably different'. He notes, too, that the practice has (or had) 'not been carried out consistently by any editor, nor has each Elizabethan form found its champion'.

One of the proper names to which Schäfer draws particular attention is that of Armado's page in *Love's Labour's Lost*, which 'occurs four times in the text and once in the stage directions in the form *Moth*'. As Schäfer says, it has been agreed for a century and more 'that the significance of the name is actually "mote"'. This is recognized by editors, but not until John Kerrigan's New Penguin edition, of 1982, has any editor been bold enough to adopt it. The same is true of the fairy with the same name in *A Midsummer Night's Dream*. 'Almost certainly', writes the new Arden editor, 'Shakespeare had in mind not "moth" but "mote", of which "moth" is a regular Elizabethan and Shakespearean spelling'.[24] He reinforces this with a number of

[23] *Studies in Bibliography* 23 (1970), 1–19.
[24] *A Midsummer Night's Dream*, ed. Harold F. Brooks, the Arden Shakespeare (London, 1979), p. 3.

Shakespearian and other references, but does not mention Schäfer and does not modernize the spelling, and so obscures a meaning which he admits to be intended, and suggests one which he regards as irrelevant.

As Schäfer remarks, it is interesting that 'Of the significant names retained in their Elizabethan forms by Clark and Wright only unobtrusive ones have been modernized. All editors have avoided changes affecting a well-known character in a noticeable way, especially since this would also mean defying the tradition of the last two hundred and fifty years.' The same is true of non-significant names. 'Petruchio', for example, in *The Taming of the Shrew*, is patently a transliteration of the Italian name now spelt 'Petruccio' (the 'cc' sounding 'tch'), just as 'Litio' (3 times) and 'Lisio' (4 times) stand for Italian 'Licio' (the 'ci' sounding 'si' or 'shi'). Only Charles Knight, I believe, adopted the Italian spelling 'Petrucio', though 'Licio', the spelling of F2, was adopted by the Cambridge editors (following Rowe) and was for a long time more generally followed. Richard Hosley argued for a return to the Folio spelling, alleging that 'Lizio' is 'an old Italian word for "garlic"', but as 'Litio' is no nearer to this than is 'Licio', and as the latter is a more Italianate form, it seems to me to be preferable.[25]

Similar examples may be adduced from other plays. In *Love's Labour's Lost*, the Q1 spellings of the names of the lords are Berowne, Longauill (15 times; also Longauil (1) and Longauile (2)), and Dumaine (15; Duman (3)). F2 spelled 'Biron' and this was common practice until the late nineteenth century. The corresponding French forms are 'Biron', 'Longueville', and 'De Mayenne'. These names well illustrate the kinds of teasing problems that face a conscientious modernizing editor. The action takes place in France (at least in so far as the action of a Shakespeare comedy can be said to take place in any particular country). Ferdinand is the King of Navarre; the Princess is the Princess of France. The natural, a priori assumption is that any French names should be modernized to their present French form unless there are good reasons for not doing so. 'Berowne' is a transliteration of the name Biron; it occurs in the Epistle to the 1594 edition of Thomas

---

[25] Hosley, note to *The Taming of the Shrew*, 2.1.60, Pelican edition (Baltimore, 1964); also discussed in his 'Sources and Analogues of *The Taming of the Shrew*', *Huntington Library Quarterly* 27 (1964), 289–308. Brian Morris, in his Arden edition (London, 1982), oddly writes 'In reading "Litio" I accept Hosley's emendation. . .' (note to 2.1.38). Murray Levith derives the name via Florio from *'litigio'* or *'litigo'*, defined by Florio as 'a plea, a pleading, a sute or controversie in lawe, debate, variance, contention' (*What's in Shakespeare's Names* (London, 1978), p. 70).

Nashe's *Christ's Tears over Jerusalem*: 'if of beere he talkes, then straight he mocks the Countie Berowne in France' (ed. McKerrow, ii.182). Richard David, in a note to his Arden edition, states that it is 'arguable that Shakespeare's intention was to *anglicize*' the French names.[26] Arguable it may be, but arguments Richard David does not adduce, and it seems to me that the burden of proof, in a play explicitly set in France, is on those who would argue that the names are *not* supposed to be French. When Shakespeare wishes to arouse English associations for his characters, he is quite capable of giving them English names, such as Nathaniel, Dull, and Costard. David also argues, in the same note, from pronunciation: 'certainly the original form of, e.g., Berowne, gives the clearer indication of how the name must be pronounced in the play (it rhymes with "moon" at IV.iii.228)'. I find this an extraordinary statement. It is my experience that people feel very uncertain how to pronounce the name, and usually make it rhyme with 'own', not with 'moon'. So I reject the argument that Q1's spelling helps to convey a necessary pronunciation, and I follow F2 in adopting the spelling which remains current to the present day. 'Longaville' and its variants represent modern 'Longueville'. So far as I know, no editor has spelt the name thus; my only hesitation in doing so was that this might inadequately suggest the necessary trisyllabic pronunciation. A French speaker would certainly give the word more than two syllables, and I see no point in pretending that this is an English name. 'Dumaine' is more difficult. Shakespeare scans as a disyllable; this, I think, implies some element of corruption along with transliteration, so in this case I retain the Quarto spelling, not, like some editors, dropping the final 'e' as its retention avoids suggesting pronunciation of the French word for 'hand'.

These are all (in Schäfer's terminology) non-significant names; still, it is not entirely without significance whether a name is, or is not, foreign, and I prefer not to flatten out Shakespeare's names into an undistinguishable non-language when they can properly be represented in a form which associates them for us with the language from which Shakespeare derived them, with which he associated them, and whose pronunciation there is, at least in many cases, evidence that he was attempting to transliterate. The same goes for scraps of foreign language in the plays. *Love's Labour's Lost* offers some particularly tiresome examples which could be discussed at great length. All I will say here is

---

[26] Arden edition (London, 1951, etc.), note 1 to *Dramatis Personae*.

that as a basic principle it seems to me right to print such passages in the correct modern form unless we think that Shakespeare is making a comic point of his character's faulty use of language. And there are at least two points where, it seems to me, an identical French phrase has been misunderstood as an English one. At 2.1.188 (Q1), Biron, speaking of his heart, says to Rosaline

> Will you prickt with your eye.

She replies:

> *No poynt*, with my knife.

And at 5.2.276-7, Maria says

> *Dumaine* was at my seruice, and his sword,
> No poynt (quoth I) my seruant, straight was mute.

Editors print 'No point' at both places, but *OED* shows that the phrase, like the much commoner *sans*, was on loan from the French. *OED* records it from 1542, with a last instance in 1610, and defines 'not a bit, not at all, not in the least'. Malone (in the Boswell-Malone edition, 1821), noting the quibble in the second instance, says 'it appears, that either our author was not well acquainted with the pronunciation of the French language, or it was different formerly from what it is at present. The former supposition appears to me much the more probable of the two.' He cites two uses where the expression is clearly felt to be French: one in the *Return from Parnassus* (1606), 'Tit, tit, tit, *non poynte*; *non debet fieri . . .*', the other from Florio's *Worlde of Words* (1598): 'Punto;—never-a whit—*no point*, as the Frenchmen say'. Though it is sometimes used with no sense of foreignness—for example by Firk in Dekker's *The Shoemaker's Holiday* (Revels edition, Scene 16, 98)— the italics in the quarto's first occurrence (repeated in F1) show that Shakespeare (probably) or the compositor thought of it as French, appropriately to the setting. So the proper modernization seems to me to be '*non point*'; a compromise pronunciation is needed to reveal the quibble on the 'point' of a knife or sword.

The question of foreignness arises, too, with certain forms of address. Consider *Love's Labour's Lost* 1.2.154, where Costard says, in Q1:

> Nay nothing M. *Moth*, but what they looke vppon.

Folio expands 'M.' to 'Master' and is followed by editors; but Costard refers to 'Monsier *Berowne*' at 4.1.53 (TLN 1029), and might possibly use the French word here, too. I should not press this, but there is a more interesting parallel example in *As You Like It*. The Folio text uses the prefix 'Monsieur' (once 'Monsieuer') nine times. It never spells out 'Master' (or 'Mister'), but has 'Mr' four times: for Corin speaking of Touchstone (3.2.12, TLN 1212) and Ganymede (3.2.76, TLN 1283), and for Touchstone speaking of Jaques (3.3.65, TLN 1681) and of Oliver Martext (3.3.85, TLN 1703). Traditionally, all four instances have been expanded to 'Master'. As Jaques is regularly addressed or referred to as 'Monsieur', and as the word is in Touchstone's vocabulary (he so addresses Le Beau at 1.2.118, TLN 296), I think it proper to expand to 'Monsieur' for the third instance. 'Master' seems more appropriate to the context at 3.2.76, TLN 1283 (Corin of 'Ganymede'), and I adopt it for the other instances, too, though rather out of the absence of a strong conviction that 'Monsieur' can be justified than as the result of any confidence that 'Master' is preferable.

Even more problems arise when serious consideration is given to the prefix usually rendered in modern editions as 'Signor' (or 'Signior', a partially modernized spelling which belongs to no current language except Shakespearianese). *OED* has main entries for four forms, all of them, it says, 'ultimately of the same etymology'. They are 'Seigneur', the French form; 'Seignior', declared to be '(1) In early use, synonymous with LORD . . . a feudal superior; the lord of a manor. Now *rare*, and chiefly as a more vernacular substitute for SEIGNEUR in speaking of a French feudal noble'; also '(2) Used to represent It. SIGNOR or F. SEIGNEUR in designations of Italians or Frenchmen'; 'Señor', 'In Spanish use or with reference to a Spaniard', first recorded in 1622; and 'Signor', 'In Italian use, or with reference to Italians'. These words are clearly defined in modern orthography but hopelessly confused in Elizabethan. It seems impossible to say for certain whether Shakespeare would have been conscious of the modern distinctions. Even in foul-paper texts the words are too close for the spelling to be of much help, though it is interesting that in *Henry V* the forms are Seigneur (6), Seignieur (1), Signeur (2), and Signieur (5) — all variants approximating to the French — while in the quarto texts of the Italianate *Merchant of Venice* and *Much Ado* the word is never spelt with an 'e' in either syllable. An old-spelling editor may, presumably must, retain the vagueness of his copy-text. But a modern-spelling editor should commit himself to one language or another, and the proper policy would seem to be to match the form to the nationality of the individual spoken of or addressed. Yet, to take one example only, the Arden editor of

Love's Labour's Lost, a play set in France, causes Don Armado, a Spaniard, to be addressed by the Italian prefix. Spaniards existed in Shakespeare's day, and were identifiable as Spaniards, even if contemporary orthography could not distinctively represent the term used in addressing them.

It would be possible to multiply instances of words where the modern foreign spelling seems preferable in a modern-spelling edition to the unmodernized, or partially modernized, or even fully modernized but English forms usually found in editions. In *All's Well that Ends Well*, for example, editors present us with someone called Gerard de Narbon, making it appear that the Countess and Lafeu speak bad French. In *As You Like It*, Orlando declares that he is 'the yongest sonne of Sir Rowland de Boys', where Shakespeare obviously intended the French word 'Bois'. Perhaps the most difficult word in this play from this point of view is the name of the forest in which much of the action occurs. In the Folio it is Arden, and so it is in all editions. There is an area of England called Arden, and there is an area of Europe called 'Ardenne'. Thomas Lodge, in the work on which Shakespeare based his play, places his action firmly in France—the story begins 'There dwelled adjoining to the city of Bordeaux a knight of most honourable parentage' —and Lodge spells the name of the forest 'Arden'. It is not, I think, arguable that this is the English 'Arden'. I see no grounds for the argument that Shakespeare transfers the action to England, and numerous reasons to believe that he intends us, in the opening scenes, to suppose that the action takes place out of England, and, specifically, in France. Orlando is 'the yongest sonne of *Sir Rowland de Boys*': a French-sounding name, whether fully modernized or not; the servant in the first scene is called Dennis: the name of the patron saint of France; Oliver addresses the wrestler as 'Mounsier *Charles*'; when Charles is asked 'Where will the old Duke liue?' he replies 'They say hee is already in the Forrest of *Arden*, and a many merry men with him; and there they liue like the old *Robin Hood* of *England*': does not the phrase 'of *England*' imply that the speakers are not in England? Soon afterwards, Oliver describes Orlando as 'the stubbornest yong fellow of France'. In the following scene, Shakespeare introduces 'Monsieur the *Beu*', and Celia addresses him in a French phrase: '*Boon-iour, Monsieur le Beu*', just as in the early scenes of *The Taming of the Shrew* odd scraps of Italian are thrown in to remind us where we are. Touchstone and Celia call Le Beau 'Monsieur', and Le Beau addresses Orlando as 'Monsieur the Challenger'; in Act Two, Scene One, the first of the forest scenes, we meet a lord of Amiens. For all these reasons, it seems to me, we should deduce that if Shakespeare had any particular place in mind as he wrote 'Arden' (however he spelt it) it is likely to have been the French forest, not the English one. The French form, Ardenne, causes no metrical problems, and so, in my view, is the one we should adopt.

I argue this case at some length because an anonymous reader, in a helpful note, has opposed this innovation. First, he argues that 'Arden is very nearly what [I, in my 'Modernizing' essay call] "an accepted anglicization of a foreign name" on the order of Rome and Milan.' This is an argument from tradition that leads to feeble-minded acquiescence in standard practice, the argument that everyone is used to it, so it's too late to change it now. If this had been accepted in musical circles, we should still be hearing *Messiah* sung by massed choirs, Bach's harpsichord works played on grand pianos, and Mozart's piano concertos played without ornamentation. It turns Shakespeare into a closed shop, a world where familiarity is more important than meaning, where we go on printing 'Signior', and 'de Boys', and 'Moth', because everyone (or nearly everyone) always (or nearly always) has.

Secondly, the reader finds that 'the location of the action . . . is a tricky question. Shakespeare drops much of the explicit Frenchness of Lodge; he has no other named locations . . . True, Shakespeare adds characters with French names (Le Beau, Jaques, Amiens), but he also adds William, Touchstone, and Martext. The characters' names range widely in linguistic origin, many of them being not national at all but conventional pastoral. The forest itself as presented boasts a combination of flora and fauna impossible for Flanders or any other single location. It is a country of the literary imagination, not an historical place of strategic importance as Calais is for *Henry V*. The place in Flanders certainly suggested the name, but the literary creation exists independently of that geographical origin, in Shakespeare's play and in English culture ever since.'

I do not dispute all this. The fact remains that Shakespeare chose for his forest a name which must have suggested either England or Flanders or both. I hope I have adduced enough arguments to show that the opening scenes, in which the forest is just mentioned, suggest a French location, that the forest of 'Arden' is distinguished from the place where Robin Hood lived, and I submit that in these circumstances it is perverse to choose a form of the word which is specifically English when a well-known Continental form is available. Certainly, Shakespeare's geography is not predominantly realistic; but it is compounded of a mixture of realities, and those that can be identified may as well be. If the identification is uncertain, here as elsewhere it is easy and proper to state that one has chosen what appears to be the primary sense, and to mention the secondary sense in a note.

Thirdly, the reader objects that the French word creates a pronunciation problem; though he admits that it 'will not affect metrics', he complains that 'a changed pronunciation will bury the allusion to the Warwickshire forest and to Shakespeare's mother'. Perhaps the allusion *should* be buried. The French pronunciation seems to me to be as capable of suggesting 'Arden' as 'Arden' can suggest 'Ardenne', and my case is based on the submission that we should prefer to suggest the primary sense. As for Shakespeare's mother, I should prefer to keep her out of sight and mind, myself, but again 'Ardenne' is not far phonologically from 'Arden'. Finally, we are told, 'Ardenne' will 'kill the slant pun on Eden—surely a deliberate slant pun (Arden is like Eden but not identical—it contains the "penalty of Adam").' Again, it seems to me that anyone who can hear a slant pun in 'Arden' and 'Eden' will hear it in 'Ardenne' and 'Eden', if perhaps at a slightly sharper angle.

This may seem a lot of pother about a single word, but it raises important questions of principle. I did not arrive at my decision light-heartedly or, I hope, light-headedly. It is not absolutely irreversible, yet. But at present it seems to me to be right, and I foresee no worthwhile future in the editing of Shakespeare unless reasoned decisions are permitted to take precedence over the claims of tradition. The claims of foreignness with which I have particularly concerned myself illustrate one of the ways in which editorial procedures may alter the nuances of a text. *Love's Labour's Lost* and *As You Like It* may emerge as more precisely French than they have previously seemed. Editorial decisions may be accused of erring on the side of over-specificity, but this seems to me preferable to the miasma of indeterminacy which hangs over texts whose editors have held back from decisions.

It is, as I said before, and as others have said before me, a difficult task that the modernizing editor undertakes. Sometimes my own instincts in favour of the status quo war with my sense of logic, and then I have to examine my instincts and try to identify the part played in them by inertia. Undoubtedly I shall fail in consistency, in some cases because I have overlooked places where my principles could have been applied, in others because I have lacked the courage to apply them rigorously, or because I have admitted grounds for exceptions inconsistently, or allowed more weight to certain considerations than others would think justifiable. Sometimes I think I ought to be more radical than I am prepared to be at present: in these moments I ask myself whether, for example, any point is served by printing 'owe' where we should say 'own', by retaining 'an' before aspirates which are now sounded (as in 'an humble') or before vowels which now have a consonantal sound (as in 'an eunuch'), or 'mine' when we should use 'my'; whether we should not print 'flee' where this would be the modern equivalent of Elizabethan 'fly'; even whether anything would be lost by abandoning obsolete inflections such as 'spake', and prefixes as in 'infortunate', 'incivil', 'unjustice', and 'ingrateful'. Certainly I should have no objection to a theatrical production in which such changes were made and I could well believe that such a production would bring me closer to Shakespeare than one in which the actors laboriously pronounced—as some of them do—'pioner' for 'pioneer', 'a' for the unemphatic 'he', 'accompt' for 'account', and 'Troyan' for 'Trojan' (as throughout the BBC television production of *Troilus and Cressida*). What I hope I have shown is that modernizing itself is not, as I was once told, merely a 'secretarial task'; that current practice leaves much room for improvement; and that when thoughtfully carried out it can yield worthwhile results.

2

EMENDING SHAKESPEARE

In lectures given in 1954 Fredson Bowers wrote, of Shakespeare's text, 'Present-day editors have long since exhausted traditional materials. Just about every emendation has been proposed that is likely to be adopted, and editing has largely resolved itself to the exercise of personal choice among the known alternatives.'[1] That is a surprisingly defeatist statement from so energetic a mind. It should be a depressing thought to anyone proposing to devote an appreciable amount of time to editing, but I believe it represents an attitude all too common among editors, and one which needs to be resisted. It is true that a present-day editor, confronted in the textual notes of editions such as the old Cambridge, the New Variorum, the new New Variorum, or the new Arden with long lists of proposed solutions for textual cruces, is likely to sigh despairingly and make his selection from among those that have already been offered, feeling often that such and such a one has usually been adopted, and that he might as well follow the tradition. Richard Proudfoot, acknowledging this attitude, offers a bracing warning against it: 'the current state of editing is one in which there is some risk of loss of editorial responsibility and alertness, such as is almost bound to arise in the frequent situation where the job does indeed involve mainly the reproduction, literatim and punctuatim, of the text of one early witness. Although this is in itself a more demanding assignment than might be supposed by those who have not attempted it, it can never be assumed that an unthinking conservatism is the right editorial position, nor even a particularly safe one. It may be preferable to uncontrolled eclecticism which does not even accept the responsibility of offering reasoned defence of its decisions, such as characterized many eighteenth- and even nineteenth-century editions of Elizabethan plays, but it falls short of paying the authors of the plays the compliment of assuming that they knew their own language and their chosen profession and of taking their plays seriously enough to verify that these are cleansed

---

[1] *On Editing Shakespeare*, p. 167.

of whatever reason can identify as most likely not to represent what they wrote.'[2]

Attempting to follow this principle—and, indeed, guided in our attempts by Richard Proudfoot, our textual adviser—my colleagues and I have had new thoughts about some of the recognized cruces, and have raised questions about certain readings that have not been previously doubted. In this chapter I have tried to choose ones for which I am responsible myself, but I have worked so closely with my colleagues that in some cases we cannot be sure to what extent each of us is responsible for a particular idea.[3]

I do not propose to offer a new set of principles of emendation; rather I should like to arrange my examples according to categories of stimulus to emendation: pointing, that is, to various features of the text that arouse suspicion of error. I start with cases where the original text makes no sense, or where doubt about the sense has caused corruption to be suspected. First, a well-known crux. In *Twelfth Night*, at the end of Act One, Scene Three, Sir Andrew shows off his talents as a dancer, and Sir Toby praises his leg. 'I,' says Sir Andrew, ''tis strong, and it does indifferent well in a dam'd colour'd stocke' (F1; TLN 242-3). Folio's 'dam'd colour'd' was first emended by Rowe, in his third edition; he read 'flame-colour'd'. Many other suggestions have been offered.[4] Charles Knight read 'damask-coloured', finding a parallel in Drayton: 'the damask-coloured dove'. Collier's alleged 'manuscript-corrector' supplied 'dun-coloured', but Dyce rejected the notion that Sir Andrew, 'a gallant of the first water, should ever dream of casing his leg in a "*dun*-coloured stock"' and reverted to Rowe, claiming that 'The epithet *flame-coloured* was frequently applied to dress. Thus, *1 Hen. IV*: I, ii, 11, "a wench in flame-coloured taffeta".' Collier retorted that 'all dispute would be at an end' only when Dyce 'produced some instance in which "flame-coloured stocks" were mentioned'. B. Nicholson (in *Notes and Queries*, 1879) also rejected 'flame-coloured' and supported the Folio reading: '"Damn'd-colour'd" is an easily understood epithet, and there is nothing against it, beyond our ignorance of the use by any one of a similar phrase in English. . . . Why cannot Sir Andrew be

[2] 'Dramatic Manuscripts and the Editor', in *Editing Renaissance Dramatic Texts*, ed. Anne Lancashire, pp. 9–38; p. 35.
[3] We are not attempting fresh historical collations. We often check those found in the standard sources, and occasionally correct them, but our search is not exhaustive and we may have missed, or misattributed, some readings.
[4] In the remainder of this paragraph I draw upon the note in H. H. Furness's New Variorum edition (1901).

allowed the imitative affectation of a word very likely to have been used,—even if it were uncommon,—among the fashion-mongers of the day?' R. M. Spence interpreted the Folio phrase as 'checkered hose'. The New Variorum editor felt that 'until some happier substitute be found', the text should remain undisturbed, adding that 'Sir Andrew's character is not so exalted as to be seriously lowered by a little pro- fanity.' The new Arden editors (Craik and Lothian, 1975) also retain F, glossing 'conceivably a gratuitous oath . . . otherwise a reference to a colour'. Yet Rowe's emendation has not been totally supplanted: it is accepted, for instance, by Kittredge and Alexander. Dover Wilson, however, followed Collier in reading 'dun', justifiably remarking that '"dunne" or "donne" might easily become "damd" through the com- mon *e:d* confusion', and claiming, less plausibly, that 'Sir Andrew is more likely to affect some ugly colour for his stockings than the bright hue in which Rowe dresses him.' He is followed by Sisson, by M. M. Mahood (New Penguin), and by Riverside; Craik and Lothian, who do not seem deeply committed to 'damned', remark that if 'dun' is right 'the humour comes from Sir Andrew's unadventurous taste in stockings'. I am not happy with either 'damned' or 'dun', and should like to add a new suggestion; 'divers-coloured' occurs in *Antony and Cleopatra*:

> On each side her,
> Stood pretty Dimpled Boyes, like smiling Cupids,
> With diuers colour'd Fannes . . .
>   (F1; 2.2.205–7, TLN 913–15)

Divers-coloured stocks would give Sir Andrew much more to boast about than 'dun-coloured' ones, and the misreading is graphically not implausible, especially if, as was common, the final 's' was written with an ascender.

Another phrase long regarded as nonsensical occurs in *Love's Labour's Lost* at 5.2.67: Rosaline is boasting of how, if she knew that Biron were 'in by th' weeke', she would torture him:

> So perttaunt like would I o'ersway his state,   .
> That he should be my foole, and I his fate. (Q1)

The quarto's 'perttaunt like' was for long regarded as unintelligible and probably corrupt. Theobald read 'pedant-like', Hanmer 'portent- like', Capell 'pageant-like'; Dover Wilson (1923) adopted a suggestion of Moore Smith and read 'planet-like', which Sisson says that he, too, had thought of, and thought well of.[5] In 1945 Percy Simpson offered

---

[5] *New Readings in Shakespeare*, 2 vols. (Cambridge, 1956), i. 121–2.

a justification of the quarto phrase on the grounds that 'paire-taunt' is the winning hand in the obsolete card game of Post and Pair.[6] Dover Wilson, in his second, 1962 edition, recording J. C. Maxwell's comment that Simpson had been anticipated by Gollancz and Herford, says 'this brilliant gloss seems at first sight irresistible'. It had been adopted by Richard David in his new Arden edition (1951), with the comment that 'Rosaline means that, whenever Berowne thinks he holds the winning cards, she will always produce a hand to beat them.' Riverside follows. Sisson, however, had offered resistance: 'I have an invincible conviction that a metaphor from a card-game would be out of place and trivial in the context'; he reverts to 'planet-like', finding it more Shakespearian, and offering palaeographical justification. Wilson, too, 'in the end' (1962) agreed with Sisson, retaining the 'planet' of his 1923 text.

I too am not convinced by Simpson's explanation. Quarto's spelling seems odd; it is true that there are many odd spellings in this quarto, but an additional objection is that the image is neither prepared for nor followed up; it seems strained to me. Nor am I attracted by 'planet-like', which seems portentous as an image and graphically implausible. My proposal is 'persuant-like': the image of a pursuivant—an officer empowered to make arrests—seems appropriate to the situation: a pursuivant would indeed 'o'ersway' someone's 'state', and so, metaphorically, become his 'fate'. The victim would then be caught: and the next words are the Princess's

> None are so surely caught, when they are catcht,
> As Wit turnde Foole . . .

and in the following line she speaks of a *warrant* such as a pursuivant would deliver:

> follie in Wisedome hatcht:
> Hath Wisedomes warrant . . .

Graphically, too, the confusion is possible ('tt' for long s plus—by a minim error—u; the word, which existed in various forms, could also be spelt with 'ceu' instead of 'su', and this might better account for the 'tt'). Though 'pursuivant' appears to have three syllables where only two are required, the resulting line is paralleled in metre by, for example, Biron's 'The sinnowy vigour of the trauayler' (4.3.308). In both cases the unstressed medial syllable (in 'pursuivant' and 'sinnowy')

---

[6] *TLS*, 24 Feb. 1945.

could be elided, and even if it were not, the result would be as acceptable metrically in the one case as the other.

Somewhat analogous is a phrase in Lance's first soliloquy in *The
Two Gentlemen of Verona*. Acting out his scene of parting with his
family, with his shoes standing in for his parents, he says, 'Now come
I to my Mother: Oh that she could speake now, like a would woman . . .'
(2.3.22 ff., TLN 619-20). Pope, as Theobald uncharitably puts it,
'unmeaningly substituted [an] *ould woman*'. 'But', Theobald continues, 'it must be writ, or at least understood, *wood woman*, i.e.
crazy, frantic with grief, or distracted, from any other cause.' On the
whole, Theobald has held the field; his emendation, says Dover Wilson,
'makes excellent sense; "wood" = mad, with a possible reference to the
wooden shoe'. Yet, as Wilson adds, it 'is not without difficulties';
Sisson concurs: it 'offers no graphic probability'.[7] Sisson (followed by
New Penguin) accepts Pope, and further emends 'now' to 'more'—
'O that she could speak more like an old woman'—which seems wanton.

This is one of the not uncommon instances where all editors agree
that emendation is necessary, but none seems entirely satisfied with
what has been offered. Casting around for a graphically plausible
alternative, I came up with 'moued'. I think no one familiar with the
Elizabethan secretary-hand would dispute that this is a probable misreading: the minims in 'm' and 'w' provide a very easy source of error,
and in secretary-hand 'e' could easily be read as 'l'. I take Lance to
mean 'O that the shoe could speak now, like a woman moved by grief':
the adjectival use of the past participle is paralleled in *Romeo and
Juliet* (1.1.86: 'heare the sentence of your moued Prince', Q2); the
word may also continue Lance's word-play: emotionally, and also
physically 'moved', as he raises the shoe. This proposal does not strike
me with the sense of total inevitability evoked by the best emendations;
but the expectation of such a feeling assumes that Shakespeare always
achieved *le mot juste*, which will therefore strike us forcibly if we
alight upon it. In this case, the word I propose seems to make rather
better sense than any of the other proposed emendations, and to be
more plausible as the source of the Folio misreading, so I shall adopt
it unless anyone suggests another which seems quintessentially
Shakespearian.

Next, a point in *Much Ado About Nothing* which has often been
questioned. Beatrice imagines the Devil turning her away from the gate

---

[7] *New Readings*, i. 54.

of hell and dispatching her to heaven: 'so' she says 'deliuer I vp my apes and away to saint Peter: for the heauens, he shewes me where the Batchellers sit, and there liue we as mery as the day is long' (Q1; 2.1.38-41). Pope emended the punctuation to read 'Peter, for the heavens;', and many editors followed suit, interpreting 'for the heavens' either as an exclamation, or as 'on my way to heaven'. In 1923 both George Sampson (in the Pitt Press Shakespeare) and Dover Wilson retained and defended Folio's punctuation. Sampson still preferred to take 'for the heavens' as an exclamation, while suggesting the alternative explanation 'for heaven', that is 'heaven being the place where there is neither marrying nor giving in marriage'. Dover Wilson noted that 'The commas of this text do not inspire much confidence, but a colon is not to be surrendered without consideration. Beatrice's heaven is where the bachelors sit.' Sisson 'would vary the reading slightly' to 'Peter. For the heavens', interpreting the passage as 'Away to Saint Peter by all means. For he shows me heaven, where the bachelors sit.'[8] The new Arden editor (1982) restores Pope's reading, citing Kittredge's note: 'Beatrice remembers . . . "for when they shall rise from the dead, they neither marry nor are given in marriage: but are as the angels which are in heaven" (*Mark* xii. 25).' No consensus has been reached, and no certainty is possible, so I feel less compunction than I otherwise might in proposing to delete Quarto's colon after Peter (which might easily have its origin in a manuscript mark of abbreviation after a shortened form of the name) and to interpret 'for' as 'fore', meaning 'before', in front of, and implying that Peter is at his traditional situation before the gates of heaven, just as Beatrice imagined the devil meeting her at the gate of hell. *OED* cites this sense as its first example of the spelling 'for', giving *All's Well* 4.4.3-4 (F1; TLN 2443-4: 'for whose throne 'tis needfull . . . to kneele') as its only example after 1300, but that seems indisputable; it may be reinforced by *Measure for Measure* 5.1.291 (F1; TLN 2672: 'for his burning throne'), and in any case a compositor might easily have printed 'for' for 'fore', which is well authenticated in this sense.[9]

A final example in this category may be given from *Antony and Cleopatra*. In Act Two, Scene Five, a hapless messenger brings Cleopatra the news that Antony has married Octavia. Cleopatra is furious: she

---

[8] *New Readings*, i. 99.
[9] According to Furness in the New Variorum edition (1899), this reading was anticipated 'as a *bare possibility*' by George Allen in manuscript notes on a copy of the play ('Philadelphia, 1867'; otherwise unidentified).

'*Strikes him downe*', '*Strikes him*', '*hales him vp and downe*', and draws a knife on him; he runs away, Charmian defends him—'The man is innocent'—and Cleopatra calls him back, promising not to bite him. Again he disclaims responsibility:

Cleo⟨patra⟩.   . . . He is married?
Mes⟨senger⟩.   I craue your Highnesse pardon.
Cleo⟨patra⟩.   He is married?
Mes⟨senger⟩.   Take no offence, that I would not offend you,
    To punnish me for what you make me do
    Seemes much vnequall, he's married to *Octauia*.
Cleo⟨patra⟩.   Oh that his fault should make a knaue of thee,
    That art not what th'art sure of. Get thee hence,
    The Marchandize which thou hast brought from Rome
    Are all too deere for me:
    Lye they vpon thy hand, and be vndone by em.

Hanmer was the first to question Cleopatra's words 'That art not what thou'rt sure of', altering 'art' to 'say'st'. This opened the floodgates. Johnson contortedly conjectured 'That art—not what?—Thou'rt sure on't.' Malone guessed that 'sure' should read 'sore'. Steevens adopted Mason's conjecture 'That art not!—What? thou'rt sure of 't!' Becket conjectured 'That thwart not . . .'. The (old) Cambridge edition, while retaining the Folio reading, records ten different additional variations on the line either conjectured or adopted by editors. The Folio reading was defended by Malone, whose explanation Dyce paraphrased as 'That art not the evil tidings of which thou givest me such assurance', and by Tollet, with a different explanation, paraphrased by Knight: 'Thou art not an honest man, of which thou art thyself *assured*, because thy master's fault has made a knave of thee.' Modern editors follow the Folio, usually accepting Malone's explanation (for example New Penguin, 'who are not as bad as the message of whose truth you are so certain'), but still sometimes betraying a lack of confidence in it: so, for example, the New Penguin editor records two earlier emendations among his list of readings 'that have often, with some plausibility, been emended', while Ridley, in the Arden edition, explains that this is 'one of those Shakespearian phrases, common in his later work, of which the sense has to be "felt" and not arrived at by syntactical analysis. Cleopatra "means" "It is the *fact* of which you are so positive that deserves my anger, and not *you*, the bringer of the news."'

This shuffling divination of Cleopatra's meaning might be acceptable if no satisfactory emendation were available, but there is an extremely

simple one that had occurred to me before I found that R. H. Case, the
original Arden editor, had mentioned it in such diffident (and mis-
printed) terms that no one had taken any notice of him; he writes
'No one seems to have conjectured "act" or [*sic*: read "for"] art.' It
is an easy graphic substitution, found in the First Quarto of *Othello*
at 3.3.332 in a reading corrected in the Folio and adopted by all
subsequent editors ('poisons,| Which at the first are scarce found to
distast. | But with a little art, [F:acte] vpon the blood, | Burne like the
mindes [F:Mines] of sulphure'). And it seems to me to produce
superior sense: Cleopatra requires the messenger to confirm the news;
he begs to be allowed not to repeat his message; she insists, even more
crossly; he pleads that she should not be offended by his reluctance
('that I would not offend you'), and provides the required information:
'he's married to *Octauia*'. To which Cleopatra responds with 'O, that
offence that he has committed would turn you into a knave—you who
do not commit the offence that you know about' ('act not' might be
understood as either 'convey the news' or 'commit Antony's fault').

Some problems of sense arise not so much from doubt about the
meaning of the words spoken as from bewilderment as to how the
scene should be staged. There is an interesting example in *Antony and
Cleopatra* (1.2). Antony has entered with the messenger who brings
news first that Fulvia had fought against Antony's brother, Lucius, then
that Labienus

> from Euphrates his conquering
> Banner shooke, from Syria to Lydia,
> And to Ionia . . .
>
> (ll. 98–100, TLN 189–91)

The Folio directs *Exit Messenger* after Antony's ashamed response to
this news, then prints

> *Enter another Messenger.*
> Ant⟨ony⟩. From *Scicion* how the newes? Speake there.
> 1. Mes⟨senger⟩. The man from *Scicion*,
>   Is there such an one?
> 2. Mes⟨senger⟩. He stayes vpon your will.
> Ant⟨ony⟩. Let him appeare:
>   These strong Egyptian Fetters I must breake,
>   Or loose my selfe in dotage.
>   *Enter another Messenger with a Letter.*
>   What are you?
> 3. Mes⟨senger⟩. *Fuluia* thy wife is dead.   (110–15, TLN 203–13)

The problem, obviously, is that according to the Folio there is only one messenger on stage when two are needed to speak. Rowe added Attendants on Antony's entry, omitted the first messenger's exit, deleted *Enter another Messenger*, and instructed the Messenger to speak 'The man from Scicion, | Is there such an one?', and an Attendant to reply. The resulting text is:

Ant⟨ony⟩. From *Scicion* how the News? speak there.
Mes⟨senger⟩. The Man from *Scicion*, is there such an one?
Attend⟨ant⟩. He stays upon your will.
Ant⟨ony⟩. Let him appear;
    These strong *Aegyptian* Fetters I must break,
    Or lose my self in Dotage. What are you?
        Enter another Messenger with a Letter.
2 Mes⟨senger⟩. *Fuluia* thy Wife is dead.

Capell also brought on Attendants with Antony; he retained the Messenger's exit and gave 'The man from *Scicion* | Is there such an one?' to the first Attendant and 'He stayes vpon your will' to the second, as well as altering and replacing the stage direction. His text reads as follows:

ANT⟨ONY⟩. From *Sicyon* how the news? Speak there.
1 A⟨ttendant⟩. The man from *Sicyon*,—Is there such a one?
2 A⟨ttendant⟩. He stays upon your will.
ANT⟨ONY⟩. Let him appear.—
    These strong *Egyptian* fetters I must break,
        Enter another Messenger.
    Or lose myself in dotage.—What are you?
Mes⟨senger⟩. *Fulvia* thy wife is dead.

Neither Rowe nor Capell sent anyone off in response to Antony's 'Let him appeare'. This became the traditional version of the scene. Ridley, however, followed F, with a rather desperate attempt to justify it:

The entering messenger finds that he has come from the wrong place, and calls to a group at the door to see whether there is another messenger who will give Antony what he wants; a second messenger in the group, eager to please, reports that there is such a messenger, waiting. I think that this perhaps gives better the general bustle of the scene, with messengers from various places coming with news, than the somewhat formal business with attendants summoning messengers in their proper turn.

This has not persuaded subsequent editors; even the Riverside edition, usually anxious to avoid emendation, adopts the Rowe-Capell arrangement. But, as Ridley says, 'the "Enter another Messenger" at line 109 [TLN 203] is obstinately there'; it should not be removed if there is any less drastic way of making sense of the passage. All that is needed, it seems to me, is to assume that Antony should speak the words 'Is there such an one?' His speech prefix might well have been omitted in the manuscript (or have been abbreviated so puzzlingly that the compositor omitted it). The compositor would then have found two adjacent speeches attributed simply to 'Messenger', and have distinguished them here and also at TLN 213 by numbers. I suggest, then, that both 'The man from *Scicion*' and 'He stayes vpon your will' should be spoken by one and the same messenger—F's *'another Messenger'*. This permits 'He stayes vpon your will' to be interpreted as a direct response to Antony, as seems most natural; it avoids assuming either that *'Enter another messenger'* is an interpolation or that it means *'Enter two messengers'*, and it permits a natural exit of the messenger at TLN 208 in response to Antony's 'Let him appeare'. Though this is not directed by the Folio, such omission is common, 'Let him appeare' is a clear instruction, and the messenger's exist turns Antony's

> These strong Egyptian fetters I must breake,
> Or loose my selfe in dotage

into a soliloquy, as seems most natural; it also avoids the simultaneous exit of three messengers, as in Ridley's version, or the need for Antony's response to the news of Fulvia's death ('There's a great Spirit gone . . .'), which follows his instruction 'forbeare me', to be spoken in the presence of attendants, as in all other editors' versions.

I have opened with examples at which the reading of the authoritative text has seemed nonsensical, or at least to make only a very strained sense. In these, an editor feels no great qualms about emending, even though he may feel a duty to record that some editors have defended the original reading. There are other points at which he may feel dissatisfied with a reading, or with a traditional emendation, which has been rarely, perhaps never, questioned, and at which indeed he may be able to offer an alternative which he regards as preferable, but where he may be inhibited from offering his own reading by the thought that the received text has seemed generally acceptable for centuries. In such cases he must wonder whether he is being super-subtle; but he has a right to express his doubts and to offer an alternative. There is, for example, a point in *The Taming of the Shrew* which has passed without comment but which seems logically weak, and which can, I think, be improved by an inoffensive, modest change. Petruccio identifies himself to Gremio:

> Borne in *Verona*, old *Butonios* [i.e. *Antonios*] sonne:
> My father dead, my fortune liues for me,
> And I do hope, good dayes and long, to see.
>   (F1; 1.2.187-9, TLN 756-8)

Why should he say 'My father dead, my fortune liues for me'? It conveys a kind of sense—'my father being dead, my money is now wholly at my disposal'—but would make much better sense if it read 'My father dead, *his* fortune lives for me.' The error is a simple one—dittographic substitution, I suppose it might be labelled—and I do not think we should be inhibited from adopting a superior reading by a fear that we might be improving on Shakespeare rather than on the agents of transmission.

Next, another passage of poor but not impossible sense from the same play, which has passed with little textual comment. At 4.4.97-9 (TLN 2286-9), Biondello dashes away from Lucentio saying 'my Master hath appointed me to goe to Saint *Lukes* to bid the Priest be readie to come against you come with your appendix'. The repetition of 'come' is, in my view, stylistically inept; and the sense is weak: why should Biondello go to the church to ask the priest to come to the church? This has bothered some editors. Keightley omitted 'to come', and H. J. Oliver (Oxford Shakespeare, 1982) cites this without adopting it. Dover Wilson, Hibbard (New Penguin), Evans (Riverside), Sisson, Heilman (Signet), and Brian Morris (new Arden) are among editors who let the original stand with neither explicit nor implicit comment. Is there, then, enough reason to feel that this is a point at which the authority of the original text is properly to be challenged? Perhaps, before replying, you will enquire what alternative I can offer. Well, at 3.2.5 of this play, Baptista anticipates with dismay the time

> when the Priest attends
> To speake the ceremoniall rites of marriage.

In *The Merry Wives of Windsor*, Anne Page, in circumstances rather similar to those in *The Taming of the Shrew*, is to be taken to be married to 'the *Deanry*, where a *Priest* attends' (F1; 4.6.31, TLN 2374). The infinitive 'to attend' might easily be compressed by assimilation; in *The Taming of the Shrew*, for example, we find 't'atchieue' (1.1.214,

TLN 525), and in *Titus Andronicus*, even more relevantly, 't'attend'
(Q1; 4.3.28).[10] In modern handwriting 'to come' and 't'attend' would
not be easily confused, but in Elizabethan secretary-hand the resem-
blance is much closer: o and a errors are common,[11] t could easily be
read as c,[12] and 'attend' could be spelt with a single 't' (*OED*); o/e is
another easy misreading, n and m have only a minim between them,
and d and e are easily confusible.[13] So I propose to read: 'my Master
hath appointed me to goe to Saint *Lukes* to bid the Priest be readie
t'atend against you come with your appendix.'

Just as logical weakness may arouse suspicion, so also may stylistic
weakness. Modern editors are very reluctant to expose themselves to
the accusation of 'improving' Shakespeare; I think that we should be
particularly on our guard when there are signs of haste in composition.
But when one perceives a stylistic weakness in a polished passage of
verse, one is entitled to question it; and if one sees a way of improving
it which might well lie behind the passage as printed, then one may
give the author the benefit of the doubt. My example is a reading that,
to the best of my belief, has not been questioned before. In *The Two
Gentlemen of Verona*, Proteus says

> Yet Writers say; as in the sweetest Bud,
> The eating Canker dwels; so eating Loue
> Inhabits in the finest wits of all.
> (F1; 1.1.42–4, TLN 46–8)

The double use of 'eating' may be deliberate, but it seems feeble to
me, even in early Shakespeare; though 'eating' is appropriate to a
'Canker', it is so only in the most figurative sense to 'Loue'. I suggest
that what stood in the manuscript was 'The eating Canker dwels; so
doting Loue . . .'. Graphically, nothing could be easier; and 'doting'
seems far more appropriate to the metaphor sustained in the subsequent lines:

> And Writers say; as the most forward Bud
> Is eaten by the Canker ere it blow,
> Euen so by Loue, the yong, and tender wit

---

[10] Fausto Cercignani, *Shakespeare's Works and Elizabethan Pronunciation*
(Oxford, 1981), p. 290, provides other examples.

[11] J. Dover Wilson, *The Manuscript of Shakespeare's 'Hamlet' and the Problems
of its Transmission*, 2 vols. (Cambridge, 1963), i. 10.

[12] Wilson, i. 111.

[13] Wilson, i. 109, 112.

> Is turn'd to folly, blasting in the Bud,
> Loosing his verdure, euen in the prime,
> And all the faire effects of future hopes.

This is one of those emendations that lay an editor open to the charge of attempting to improve on Shakespeare, but I like to think that in making it I am merely improving on his compositors, or on Ralph Crane's transcription of Shakespeare's handwriting.

An editor's first duty is, if possible, to make sense of the original text, even if he then decides to alter it. Having offered passages where I think that nonsense, or weak sense, can be improved upon on the assumption of rectifiable error, I want now to offer two in which I think that common emendations are unnecessary because they assume deficiency of sense where the original reading is in fact intelligible.

At 4.3.243 of *Love's Labour's Lost* the King says 'By heauen, thy Loue is blacke as Ebonie.' Biron replies:

> Is Ebonie like her? O word deuine!
> A wife of such wood were felicitie. (Q1)

The (old) Cambridge edition has the interesting note: 'Theobald's note is: "*O* word *divine!* This is the reading of all the editions that I have seen; but both Dr Thirlby and Mr Warburton concurred in reading (as I had likewise conjectured) *O* wood *divine!*" "Wood," however, is the reading of Rowe's first edition. It was perhaps only a happy misprint, as it is altered to "word" in the second.' Dover Wilson's only comment is 'The emendation is accepted by all.' Richard David, Sisson, and Evans (Riverside) do not comment. But is the emendation (whether deliberate or not) a 'happy' one? Granted, 'wood' is perfectly good sense; 'ebony' is indeed a 'wood', but it is also a 'word', just as Romeo is a name as well as a Montague; indeed Biron himself is soon to say

> For Wisedomes sake, a worde that all men loue:
> Or for Loues sake, a worde that loues all men . . .
>
> (ll. 353–4)

The emendation works in the direction of the commonplace, and I think it should be abandoned.

Secondly, a passage in *Much Ado About Nothing* which has been frequently though unnecessarily emended, and which, I suggest, is incorrectly glossed by those editors who defend the Quarto reading. In Act Three, Scene Two, Don Pedro and Claudio are joking about Benedick, in his presence:

Claud⟨io⟩. And when was he woont to wash his face?
Prince Yea or to paint himselfe? for the which I heare what they
    say of him.
Claud⟨io⟩. Nay but his iesting spirit, which is now crept into a
    lute-string, and now gouernd by stops.

(Q1; ll. 50–4)

In 1859, W. S. Walker, in his *Critical Examination of the Text of Shakespeare*, proposed 'new-governed'. This was adopted by Dyce and others. Boas conjectured instead 'new-crept'; this was adopted by Dover Wilson and some later editors. Both readings assume (as does *OED*) that *stops* refers to the frets on a *lute*, so that there is no disjunction between *now crept* and *now gouerned*. A. R. Humphreys, in his new Arden edition, does not emend, but also assumes that 'The *stops* are the frets, the points at which the string is *governed*, or stopped, by the finger on the finger-board.' His paraphrase is 'Benedick's spirit does not now run freely; it is repeatedly checked.' But this makes little sense of the repetition of *now*, which one would expect to be antithetical (*OED* 7), meaning 'at some times ... at other times'; indeed, Riverside records the emendation 'new-crept', saying that 'some editors' adopt it 'in view of the second *now* in the sentence.'

Difficulties disappear if we accept the explanation offered in a neglected, 'Parallel Passages' edition of the play by A. G. Newcomer (Stanford, California, 1929), where 'stops' is referred to the recorder, not the lute, with ample supporting evidence from Shakespeare, of which the most relevant is 'gouerne these ventages with your fingers, & the vmber ['thumb', F] . . . looke you, these are the stops' (*Hamlet*, Q2; 3.2.349–51). It is interesting, too, that, discounting this passage in *Much Ado*, Shakespeare nowhere uses 'stop' or 'stops' of a stringed instrument. The passage means, then, that Benedick's *jesting spirit* at times conceals itself in a lute string, and at other times permits itself to be played on (in, by implication, a melancholy fashion) like the finger-holes of a recorder. The lute was especially associated with lovers' serenades, and the recorder is here thought of as a purveyor of sad, or *heavy*, music—'Indeed that tells a heauy tale for him' is Don Pedro's response to Claudio's remark. Claudio is speaking of Benedick in terms which Benedick had earlier used of him: 'I haue knowne when there was no musique with him but the drumme and the fife, and now had he rather heare the taber and the pipe' (Q1; 2.3.11-13).

In the instances given so far, the sense of the original may be suspected of corruption in the process of transmission. I turn now to points at which the blame for inconsistency, poor sense, or nonsense, is likely to be Shakespeare's own. The distinction is made by Greg: 'An editor should of course remove so far as possible all errors and imperfections for which there is reason to believe either a scribe or compositor responsible.' He footnotes this with the statement: 'There can be no doubt that Shakespeare occasionally wrote a sentence that does not mean what he intended, though at the time of writing he evidently thought that it did. Sometimes it means the exact opposite: e.g. *Macbeth* III.vi.8-10, "Who cannot want the thought, how monstrous It was ... To kill their gracious father?"'[14] But Greg betrays a certain, uncharacteristic shiftiness about what the editor should do in such cases. In his text he continues 'indeed, he may be allowed to rectify any blunder which it is certain that the author would have recognized as such had it been pointed out to him, provided that neither the nature of the blunder nor the form of the correction is open to doubt. The postulate is not intended to allow the "correction" of irregular metre or grammar or the removal of inconsistencies that the author overlooked and may indeed have regarded as permissible or insignificant, nor yet of the more definite errors we sometimes find woven into the texture of a play.' Clearly Greg was experiencing difficulty in general legislation—this is part of his 'Rule 1'—and I think, as *he* probably thought in practice, that each case needs to be taken individually, especially because it is rarely possible to discount completely the chance of imperfect transmission. For example, Greg would not permit 'the removal of inconsistencies that the author overlooked and may indeed have regarded as permissible or insignificant'. Let us look at one or two cases.

In the first and fifth speeches of the Quarto text of *Much Ado About Nothing* Leonato speaks of 'Don Peter'. Throughout the rest of the play this character is called Don Pedro. Editors have regularly followed Rowe in adopting this form throughout; as the new Arden editor writes, 'Shakespeare probably at first [intended] to anglicize Bandello's "Piero" and then, since the Prince is Aragonese, [settled] for the Spanish form.' This is a foul-papers text; Shakespeare might well have regarded the inconsistency as 'insignificant', but it also seems likely that he would have recognized it as a 'blunder ... had it been pointed

---

[14] *The Editorial Problem*, p. xi.

out to him', and I see no reason to quarrel with standard editorial practice. But there is a very similar situation in a different play where editors have not regularized. The heroine of *All's Well that Ends Well* is called Helena four times in the Folio; three of these occurrences are in stage directions, only one in dialogue, a prose passage in the opening scene: 'No more of this *Helena*, go too . . .' (1.1.44–5; TLN 53). The occurrences in stage directions are in the opening direction and in two others in Act Two, Scenes Four and Five (TLN 1209, 1325). The short form of her name—Hel⟨l⟩en—occurs twenty-five times, sixteen of them in dialogue, both verse and prose. It seems that Shakespeare was initially rather inconsistent but that he eventually abandoned the long form; again, this is a foul-papers text, and if in *Much Ado* Peter becomes Pedro, it seems as logical to alter the one occurrence in dialogue, along with the three in directions, of 'Helena' to 'Helen'. This is likely to encounter resistance, I suspect, because editors have always printed the longer form in their character-lists, no doubt simply because it occurs first in the play. But, even if we might allow an insignificant variant in the dialogue, it is surely right at least to recognize that the predominant form is Helen, and to refer to the character by this name.

A more complex case occurs in *Julius Caesar*, in which the Folio text at various points uses Italianate forms of Roman names. 'Antonio' occurs five times, 'Antonius' not at all; 'Claudio' six times, 'Claudius' not at all; 'Flavio' once, 'Flavius' five times; 'Octavio' twice, 'Octavius' twenty-three times. Almost all editors have regularized all occurrences to the standard Latin form, just as they have also altered 'Varrus' (which occurs once in dialogue, twice in directions) to the paradoxically superior Latin form 'Varro'. These standardizations, almost universally accepted, are far more drastic than that of 'Helena' to 'Helen', which has not so far been made. They were resisted by Maurice Charney in his Bobbs-Merrill edition (Indianapolis and New York, 1969), who says that he has 'chosen the ironically radical expedient of giving [the names] as they appear in the Folio' (p. xxxvii). He suggests that 'these Italianate endings are colloquial variants of the more formal Latin nominatives (Antonius, Octavius, and Flavius)'. He is followed by the Riverside editor, and I am inclined to follow suit, too, not because, as Evans writes, 'there is no reason to doubt that they represent what Shakespeare actually wrote'—that would justify the retention of indifferent spelling variants—but because they are distinct forms of the names and to classicize them is to treat Shakespeare's language in the same way as to correct his anachronisms would be to change his content. It is not quite the same as it would be to change Celia's 'my sweet *Rose*, my deare *Rose*' (*As You Like It* 1.2.19-20, TLN 191) to 'my sweet Rosalind, my dear Rosalind', because there the familiar form reflects the speaker's relationship and attitude to the person addressed, whereas here the variation appears to reflect Shakespeare's frequent indifference to the form used. But that indifference is as revealing as the fact that, in this play, though he refers regularly to Marcus Brutus and Marcus Cato, he consistently uses the familiar 'Mark Antony', not 'Marcus Antonius' (which, incidentally, does occur, once, in *Antony and Cleopatra*). No one would wish, if metre permitted it, to alter Mark Antony to Marcus Antonius; if we do not alter the English form, why alter the Italian?—especially since its persistence over a group of names suggests that Shakespeare would have been unlikely to adopt the classical form throughout in revising the play—as, on the other hand, he might well have regularized the single instance in dialogue of 'Helena'. So in this matter I agree with Charney and Evans.

There are points at which Shakespeare seems to have committed inconsistencies of plotting which are easily ironed out and where an editor may reasonably feel justified in making the correction. In *The Winter's Tale*, for example, Time, the Chorus, tells us that the gap in the action has lasted 'sixteene yeeres' (F1; 4.1.6, TLN 1585) but a few lines later Camillo says 'It is fifteene yeeres since I saw my Countrey' (4.2.3, TLN 1617). That sixteen is the right figure seems to be confirmed later: Paulina says that the 'Caruers excellence ... lets goe-by some sixteene yeeres' (5.3.30-1, TLN 3220-1) and a little later (l. 50, TLN 3243) Camillo says that 'sixteene Winters cannot blow away' Leontes' sorrow. On the whole, modern editors do not rectify the inconsistency, and many do not even mention it; but if, as is not impossible, the number had been written in roman numerals, misreading would have been easy, and I should follow the first Oxford editor in emending 'fifteene' to 'sixteen'. Similarly in *Measure for Measure*, at, 1.2.161 (TLN 261) Claudio remarks that 'ninteene Zodiacks haue gone round' since the laws of Vienna were properly enforced, but at 1.3.21 (TLN 311) the Duke gives the period as 'this foureteene yeares'. Confusion between 'xiv' and 'xix' would have been easy; perhaps the shorter period is more plausible, so Theobald's proposed alteration of Claudio's 'ninteene' to 'fourteen' is acceptable.

This is an example of a little, localized problem which can easily be set right with no damage to metre or rhyme. Other, related cases are more tricky. In *The Two Gentlemen of Verona*, for instance, there is

much apparent geographical confusion. In a prose passage at the beginning of Act Two, Scene Five, Lance, who is in Milan, welcomes Speed
to Padua. There is general agreement that Pope should be followed
in emending to 'Milan'; I suggest that perhaps 'Padua' is a first thought,
rejected but not cancelled in the manuscript; Padua had a famous
university to which Valentine might appropriately have been sent.
That emendation is easily made; slightly more difficult is the statement
made by the Duke of Milan when he is clearly on home ground, 'There
is a Lady in *Verona* heere | Whom I affect' (3.1.81-2; TLN 1150-1).
The anomaly looks like an authorial oversight, possibly a remnant of
an early draft. Some editors, including the Riverside, read 'Milano'
(first suggested by Collier; Pope had read 'Milan'), which I find a little
fanciful, especially as the form does not occur in the Folio text. I prefer
Halliwell's 'of Verona', and I think it is right to make one change or
the other even though to do so contravenes Greg's rule that 'the form
of the correction' should not be 'open to doubt'. Still more difficult
is 5.4.128-9 (TLN 2253-4), where Valentine threatens Thurio: 'Doe
not name *Siluia* thine: if once againe, | *Verona* shall not hold thee.'
Verona does not hold Thurio here, and, so far as we know, never did.
'Milan' must be meant. Theobald changed to 'Milan shall not behold
thee', presumably changing 'hold' to 'behold' in order to rectify the
metre. Riverside reads 'Milan', attributing to Theobald, but retains
'holds', which leaves the line unmetrical; it would have seemed more
logical to follow Collier here, too, with 'Milano'. In this case, perhaps
illogically, I prefer not to make a change while noting the problem
and suggesting that in performance 'This Milan' or 'Our Milan' might
be substituted. For some reason—perhaps because an edition can be
annotated—one is more willing to confront a reader than a playgoer
with nonsense.

Now, a passage in *Love's Labour's Lost* where I am not sure whether
or not there is a logical difficulty. Armado, Mote, Holofernes, and
Nathaniel are discussing the entertainment that they propose to present.
'Shall I tell you a thing?' says Armado. 'We attende', replies Holofernes.
'We will haue', says Armado, 'if this fadge not, an Antique' (Q1; 5.1.127).
'To fadge' means 'to come off', 'to succeed'; editors gloss 'fadge not'
as 'fail', 'turn out badly', etc. but do not explain the meaning of the
sentence in context. My difficulty is in understanding why Armado
should apparently be looking forward to a fiasco. This assumes that
by 'Antique' he means the show they are planning; and he has no
apparent reason to use 'Antique' pejoratively. An alternative possibility

is that he means that if the proposed pageant fails, they will have something else, 'an Antique' (perhaps the dialogue of the Owl and the Cuckoo which ends the play); but the build-up to the statement—'Shall I tell you a thing?'—seems to me to suggest that he is looking forward with exultation to success, not failure: 'If this comes off, we shall have a really good show.' As he *wants* an 'antic'—'the King would haue me present the Princesse (sweete chuck) with some delightfull ostentation, or show, or pageant, or antique, or fierworke' (5.1.94-6), he should be saying 'if this fadge', not 'if this fadge not'. So I propose to read 'fadge now' (rejecting 'faile not' on the principle of *difficilior lectio*) unless someone persuades me that the Quarto reading can be satisfactorily explained as it stands.

Many of the proposed emendations to be found among the textual notes to editions of Shakespeare are the result of attempts to mend his metre; and many of these that were once to be found in the text are now relegated to the textual notes, or are quietly forgotten altogether. Metrical emendation has become unfashionable. This is in part a beneficial result of increased understanding of Shakespeare's metrics. No one now would wish to follow Pope in changing Macbeth's 'Now o'er the one half-world' to 'Now o'er one half the world', or Hamlet's 'To hide the slain. O, from this time forth', to 'To hide the slain. O then from this time forth', or his 'To tell my story. What warlike noise is this' to 'To tell my tale. What warlike noise is this.' Nevertheless the policy of refusing to mend metre can be, and I think has been, taken too far. We should pay our poet the compliment of assuming that he cares for metrical values, and be willing to emend when the surviving text is demonstrably deficient. Gary Taylor is carrying out a metrical analysis of each Shakespeare play as we edit it, and this is proving very helpful in suggesting the varying metrical norms at different stages of Shakespeare's career. Here I want just to give a few instances of cases where I have felt that emendation on metrical grounds is desirable even though some modern editors disagree.

An example is in *Twelfth Night*. Viola says

> She made good view of me, indeed so much,
> That me thought her eyes had lost her tongue . . .
>   (F1; 2.2.17-18, TLN 675-6)

The Arden editors remark 'The metre, and presumably the text, is defective, but . . . it is impossible to choose between "sure" (F2's emendation, perhaps suggested by 1. 20) and "as" (Walker's conjecture);

Furness ... defends the irregularity.' Is this not an abnegation of editorial responsibility? The editors agree that emendation seems necessary, but do not emend because they cannot choose between two alternative emendations that have already been made. They give no sign of having tried to think of a fresh one. They say that the irregularity has been defended, but the fact that they neither cite the grounds of the defence nor offer anything of their own to support it suggests lack of confidence in it. Some other modern editors, too (for example New Penguin, Riverside) let the original reading stand, these without comment; while others adopt one of the two emendations cited. The nub of the problem that appears to have inhibited the Arden editors from emending is, I suspect, not so much the difficulty of choice between the alternatives suggested as the fact that the line makes sense without emendation, so any addition inevitably seems like padding. Nevertheless, I agree with them and the many other editors who feel that Shakespeare is unlikely to have written the line as it stands in the Folio. Walker's 'as methought' has no parallel in Shakespeare (nor does 'as methinks' occur). F2's 'sure methought' is, of course, without authority, and Shakespeare's usage elsewhere supports a temporal rather than an intensive adverb, so I propose 'that soon methought'; 'soon' also has the advantage of seeming a little less like mere padding than the other proposals.[15]

A line which has been even more generally agreed to be faulty yet which often goes unemended is 3.1.4 of *The Taming of the Shrew*. Lucentio, Hortensio, and Bianca are on stage. Lucentio rebukes Hortensio for growing 'too forward'. Hortensio retorts

> But wrangling pedant, this is
> The patronesse of heauenly harmony . . .

The new Arden editor, like most others, avoids emendation, while stating unequivocally 'The line is in some way incomplete.' He continues, correctly, 'Various attempts have been made to expand it, but none is more than guesswork', and recommends Theobald's proposal to insert 'This is a shrew' at the beginning of the line as being 'as good as any'. One sympathizes with modern editors' reluctance to emend. The Oxford Shakespeare editor makes the same decision, while being more willing to believe that the line may be undamaged: it 'is certainly

---

[15] Richard Proudfoot, agreeing with this argument but finding 'soon' not urgent enough, plausibly proposes 'straight'.

short, and hard to scan, but it is not hard to say, and makes sense as it stands'. I have to dissent from that judgement. It is, perhaps, just conceivable that this line belongs in the category I mentioned earlier, of those that Shakespeare may have left in a rough state in the haste of composition—this is, we believe, a foul-papers text—and which he would have wished to improve before regarding the play as finished. The Cambridge editors even make the interesting point that the line scans (roughly) if the speech prefix is included, and they take this as a sign of hasty composition. But the lines before and after this one are regular enough, and I think that the editor should chance his arm at an emendation. Rejecting Theobald's suggestion, along with Hanmer's 'Know this lady is', Malone's 'this lady is', Collier's 'Tut! wrangling pedant, I avouch this is', Elze's conjectured 'Her sister—tut! But wrangling pedant this is', and Tillyard's suggested 'this Urania is', I have accepted Gary Taylor's suggestion of 'this Bianca is', which both rectifies the metre and provides the desirable antithesis with Katherine:

Luc⟨entio⟩. . . . Haue you so soone forgot the entertainment
     Her sister *Katherine* welcom'd you withal.
Hort⟨ensio⟩. But wrangling pedant, this *Bianca* is,
     The patronesse of heauenly harmony.

Somewhat similar is a line in *Titus Andronicus*. Threatening Lavinia, Demetrius says to Tamora:

> This minion stood vpon her chastitie,
> Vpon her Nuptiall vow, her loyaltie,
> And with that painted hope, braues your mightenes,
> And shall she carrie this vnto her graue.
>   (Q1; 2.3.124–7)

J. C. Maxwell, in his original Arden edition (1953), followed the Quarto while pointing out that the 'rhythm' of the third line 'is very awkward'. He remarked that 'The insertion of *she* makes the line an acceptable Alexandrine', and glossed 'painted' as 'specious', while recording T. M. Robertson's conjectural emendation to 'fals'd'. In his revised edition (1961) he still follows Q1, remarks that 'Metre and sense' are awkward, abandons his proposed insertion, drops his gloss on 'painted' and Robertson's conjecture, but records Alice Walker's proposal 'pall'd', meaning 'weakened'. It did not inspire him with enough confidence to emend. The Riverside editor similarly followed Q while betraying his uncertainty with a note on 'painted': 'unreal.

False. The line may be corrupt', and by recording F2's addition following 'hope' of 'she' (also added, though not collated, by the old Arden editor). The collations in the Cambridge edition show many attempts to mend both metre and sense. It is characteristic of modern practice that editors recognize the problem while shying away from the attempt to solve it. My proposal is 'quainte' for 'painted'. This is metrically acceptable. The sense seems good—'fastidious', 'fine' (derisorily)—and the error may be explained by the supposition that a compositor, finding the initial letters difficult to read, guessed at 'painte' and turned it into a past participle to fit the context. Something of a parallel is provided by *1 Henry VI* 4.1.102-3: 'though he seeme with forged queint conceite | To set a glosse vpon his bold intent.'

As a final category, I should like to mention a number of points at which the precise reading of a modern-spelling text, while not strictly involving emendation of the sense, has some of the force of an emendation as the result of the editor's interpretation of what is printed in the original text.

I start with one for which we are indebted to A. L. Rowse. He communicated it in a letter to the *Times Literary Supplement* on 18 July 1952, pointing out that when, in *Love's Labour's Lost*, Dull responds to Holofernes's 'Sir *Nathaniel, haud credo*' with 'Twas not a *haud credo*, twas a Pricket' (Q1; 4.2.10-12), Dull is demonstrating his ignorance of Latin by understanding *haud credo* as 'auld grey doe'. Everyone now accepts this, but no editor so far has acted on it in the logical way, which is to print 'auld grey doe' when that is Dull's meaning. This would not, perhaps, be appropriate in an old-spelling edition, but in a modern-spelling text where it is customary and, I think, proper to spell according to the primary sense, it seems right to me.

Another phrase in the same scene is capable of a new interpretation which does not require actual emendation. Holofernes (Nathaniel in Q1 and F1), addressing Jaquenetta, asks 'But *Damosella virgin*, Was this directed to you?' (Q1; 4.2.121-2). '*Damosella virgin*' is usually interpreted simply as a tautologous form of address and passed over (as by Dover Wilson, Arden, Pelican, and Riverside) without comment. '*Damosella*' may be a meaningless affectation, but the passage gains in meaning and in appropriateness to its speaker if it is treated as Holofernes's version of the (medieval) Latin 'domicella' followed by his condescending translation of it for his hearer's benefit: 'but, *domicella*—virgin [to you] —, was this directed to you?'

Interpretation can also help to solve a difficult problem shortly before this, in the same play. (I may say that this example is one that would have fitted into at least two of my preceding categories, as the original reading seems poor sense and also raises suspicions about the logic of Shakespeare's plotting; but I include it here because an element in the proposed new reading involves not emendation but reinterpretation of an undisputed reading.) Costard, alone, is gloating over what he regards as his triumph over Boyet.

> By my soule a Swaine, a most simple Clowne.
> Lord, Lord, how the Ladies and I haue put him downe.
> O my troth most sweete iestes, most inconie vulgar wit,
> When it comes so smoothly off, so obscenly as it were, so fit.
> *Armatho* ath toothen side, o a most daintie man,
> To see him walke before a Lady, and to beare her Fann.
> To see him kisse his hand, & how most sweetly a wil sweare:
> And his Page atother side, that handfull of wit,
> Ah heauens, it is [a] most patheticall nit.

$$\text{(Q1; 4.1.133–41)}$$

Editors have suspected that the last five lines are misplaced. Richard David, in the Arden edition, asks, rhetorically, 'What are they [that is, Armado and his page] doing in this scene? We must suppose that they took part in it in an earlier draft.' This perhaps derives from Dover Wilson's note, which comments that 'Dyce and Staunton point out that these lines are "utterly irrelevant to anything in the scene"' and also suggests that the anomaly is the result of revision.

As I am reluctant to attribute unintentional nonsense to Shakespeare, my first thought was to try to find a point in the play where the lines would fit better, and to move them there, or else to put them in an appendix along with the first drafts of passages which are acknowledged to exist in both revised and unrevised states. But then I realized that all difficulties disappear if we alter a single letter, easily misread, and take a word in one of its recorded senses rather than another. The crucial phrase is in the fifth of these lines: '*Armatho* ath toothen side.' Attention has centred on the second and third words; the old Cambridge edition, following Rowe, printed them as 'o' th' one'. Wilson supposed that Shakespeare 'wrote "Arm ath toothon", inadvertently dividing "Armath", so that the compositor took "Arm" for the contraction and expanded it: "toothon" became "toothen" by an $o:e$ misprint, and "toothon" is not at all an impossible form . . .'. Wilson therefore prints 'Armado to th'one side', and is followed by Arden and Signet.

Essentially, these two interpretations have held sway, though with variations; Kittredge printed 'o' th' t'one side'; Alexander is almost identical with 'a th' t'one side'; Sisson does not discuss the problem, and prints 'a th' one' which is also Riverside's version (attributing to Rowe); Pelican (Harbage himself) has 'o' th' t'one side'.

It is clear from all this fiddling that editors have worried about the Quarto spelling, but among the ones I have cited (some, of course, without the opportunity to annotate), none faces the problem stated by the Arden editor: 'What are they [Armado and Mote] doing in this scene?' Why does Costard, after talking about Boyet, suddenly, with no transition, have a vision of Armado and his page walking side by side? What I regard as my moment of illumination came when I turned from 'ath toothen' to the word 'side' and read in *OED* (IV, 17b, examples from 1300 to 1732) that the word could be used as the equivalent of 'hand' in the modern phrase 'on the other hand'. As Dover Wilson recognized, editors' interpretations involve the emendation of 'e' to 'o': 'en' is not likely to represent 'one', even in a colloquial corruption. If, instead of emending 'e' to 'o', we emend 'n' to 'r', we get 'ath toother', a form closely paralleled in *Troilus and Cressida* 5.4.7–8: 'Ath' tother side, the pollicie of those craftie swearing raskalls . . .' (Q1). So, with no more emendation than in the traditional, though still nonsensical, reading we have a phrase which makes the passage entirely comprehensible, 'ath toother side', modernized to 'o' th'other side', and glossed 'on the other hand', becoming the linking phrase between Costard's contempt of Boyet and his praise of Armado: a comparative judgement which acts as a comic comment on Costard himself.[16]

I conclude with a reading which, though it is purely the interpretation of a spelling, nevertheless has the force of an emendation, and which I hope may serve as an example of the ways in which a modernizing editor is pushed to examine the text more closely than an old-spelling editor might find necessary, and in which a modern-spelling edition can convey a sense which, apparently, has not been recognized by all those who have read the text in old spelling. It occurs in *Titus Andronicus*. The Nurse has brought to Aaron his new-born child with the message that its mother, Tamora, would have it put to death. Aaron rejects the demand:

[16] However one glosses or emends the phrase its virtual repetition – '*Armatho ath toothen side . . . his Page atother side*' – is awkward. Presumably the two phrases are used in the same sense, Costard contrasting first Armado with Boyet, then the 'nit' Mote with Armado.

Tell the Empresse from mee I am of age
To keepe mine owne, excuse it how shee can.
Demetrius. Wilt thou betray thy Noble Mistris thus.
Aron. My Mistris is my Mistris, this my selfe,
    The vigour, and the picture of my youth:
                    (Q1; 4.2.104–8)

In what sense, I asked myself, is the baby the 'vigour' of Aaron's youth? Most editors pass the line by without comment. Schmidt glosses 'vigour' here as 'force, strength', but this seems excessively proleptic. Dover Wilson notes 'Characteristic Sh⟨akespearian⟩ hendiadys'. But *OED* records 'vigour' as a southern Middle English variant of 'figure' and records it as a thirteenth- and fourteenth-century variant spelling; initial 'v' for 'f' remained in dialect pronunciation, as Dobson shows,[17] and Joseph Wright specifically records 'vigure' (for 'figure') in the West Country as late as the nineteenth century. I think we achieve better sense by understanding, and modernizing to, 'The figure and the picture of my youth', and that this is fully supported by the linguistic evidence. I have not found an exact parallel for 'figure and picture', but *OED*'s quotations include, for example, 'the similitude and fygure of the passage of the chyldren of Israel from Egypte' (*sb.*, 21b, 1526), 'Ryche pictures where as were fygured many a noble hystory' (*v.*, 2; *c.*1500), and 'He never ... refused to suffer himself to be painted or figured out in a Statue' (*v.* 15b, 1657). 'Figure' is capable of many shades of meaning; 'figure and picture' is roughly tautologous, but might be glossed 'embodiment and representation' or 'image and likeness'; the baby is, as Lucius later remarks to Aaron, 'This growing image of thy fiend-like face' (5.1.45).

[17] *English Pronunciation 1500-1700*, 2 vols. (Oxford, 1957; 2nd edn. 1968), §357.

3

THE EDITOR AND THE THEATRE:
EDITORIAL TREATMENT OF STAGE
DIRECTIONS

An editor of plays faces problems deriving specifically from the fact that he is editing works written for the theatre. Such problems are not confined to Shakespeare, though they are probably present in as acute a form in his works as in those of any other dramatist of the period, mainly because Shakespeare seems to have had no interest in preparing his plays for the reader. By 'reader' here I do not mean simply one who wished to read a play, whether or not he saw it; I mean even those who were obliged to read it as part of their duty to put it upon the stage.

It is clear from all the available evidence that Shakespeare wrote, not as a dramatist whose work would be completed at the moment that he delivered his script to the company for which it was written, but as one who knew that he would be involved in the production process. As a result, there is frequently little attempt in the scripts that survive to objectify many aspects of the imagined performance which would nevertheless have had to be communicated to the performers before the play could exist on the stage. Shakespeare must have been confident that he could influence the production process by word of mouth—probably as, indeed, a figure equivalent to that of the modern director;[1] and he must have known, too, that he could rely on the assistance of fellow-members of his company with more or less technical matters such as the provision of music cues and the design—or the choice from existing stock—of costumes and properties. We know from the evidence of a few actors' names surviving in the speech prefixes of texts printed from foul papers that occasionally, at least, Shakespeare had specific actors in mind as he wrote, because sometimes he absent-mindedly wrote the actor's name instead of the character's. The clearest instance is in Act Four, Scene Two, of *Much Ado About Nothing*, where the Quarto frequently uses the actors'

---

[1] See, for example, David Klein, 'Did Shakespeare Produce his own Plays?', *Modern Language Review* 57 (1962), 556–60.

names '[Will] Kemp' (sometimes abbreviated) and '[Richard] Cowley' for Dogberry and Verges.[2] There must have been many more such cases for which no evidence has survived, and even if Shakespeare did not care exactly who played a particular role, he would have been on hand to convey his wishes about such important, sometimes vital matters as the character's age and appearance. Similarly, it is clear that he felt no need systematically to write instructions for action or movement. His prime concern as he wrote was the words to be spoken, with providing a script from which the individual performers' parts could be copied. In the earlier stages of composition, at least, he was so overridingly preoccupied by thoughts of what the characters should say that he could content himself with the sketchiest of stage directions, sometimes even omitting to indicate that a character should be present, frequently omitting to indicate when he should leave, sometimes not even bothering too much about who should speak particular lines or about providing dialogue to cover necessary action.

The result of this method of composition was a script from which no one other than the author himself could even have transcribed actors' parts with any confidence that he was providing correct cues for entries, words to be spoken, and exits, let alone any information about details of staging. Anyone doubting this should try transcribing the parts for Act Three, Scene Three—the first Watch scene—of *Much Ado About Nothing* from the Quarto, and putting them into rehearsal with no information other than that provided by the text as printed, in which we are not told how many watchmen should appear, in which a general *Exeunt* is marked when in fact the Watch must remain on stage, and in which nine speeches are ascribed simply to 'Watch'—that is, with no indication of *which* watchman should speak—and in which George Seacoal is 'Watch 2' at his first appearance, and 'Watch 1' later in the scene. Confusion would undoubtedly follow.

We cannot, I think, say for certain whether Shakespeare ever handed over to his company a script in so unfinished a state. The 'foul papers' of which it consisted may have been revised and transcribed by himself, or by someone else under his direction, before anyone was expected to prepare the actors' parts. But we do know that such scripts found their way into the printing house, and that the compositors' attempts to make sense of them are all that the modern editor—and so the modern director—has to go on in his attempt to determine and

---

[2] See also Greg, *The Shakespeare First Folio*, pp. 114-16.

realize Shakespeare's intentions. I have written elsewhere about such texts, with particular attention to *Much Ado About Nothing* and the editorial and theatrical problems consequent upon its derivation from foul papers,[3] so I will touch only lightly on the topic here.

While texts printed from foul papers tend to be the most sketchy and inconsistent in their directions, texts of different origin present different problems. Certain Folio texts, for instance, were printed from transcripts—whether of the author's holograph manuscripts or of transcribed prompt-books—made, we believe, by the King's Men's scrivener Ralph Crane. Crane had an irritating tendency to list at the head of a scene all the characters taking part in it, with no concern for the particular point in the scene at which they should make their entrance. He was also liable to incorporate 'his impressions of the action in the phrasing of the directions', to revise their language, and to 'suppression of directions for action within scenes' (as almost completely in *The Two Gentlemen of Verona*).[4] Crane's placing of directions can cause problems: 'All interior entrances in his dramatic transcripts were written to the right of dialogue, and were not centred or otherwise conspicuously marked.' And 'because he inserted them after writing the dialogue, they could be misplaced. At the least, the compositors, who often centred entrances within a scene on the width of the column, could mistake the correct place for their insertion.'[5]

Other texts in the Folio are printed from prompt-books in which information or directions emanating from the theatre have, with greater or lesser degrees of consistency, been added to the script that Shakespeare handed over. It is not always easy to identify such texts with any certainty, mainly because an experienced playwright, however slapdash he may have been in his foul-paper stage of composition, might, in making a fair copy, have tidied up his directions no less than the dialogue, and would have been familiar with the technical language of the theatre. But it seems probable that the Folio texts of *Julius Caesar*, and *Macbeth*, at least (as well as the quarto *Two Noble Kinsmen*), were printed from prompt copy.

The situation is additionally complicated by the fact that a number of Shakespeare's plays exist in two versions, one apparently representing

[3] 'Editorial Treatment of Foul-Paper Texts: *Much Ado About Nothing* as Test Case', *Review of English Studies* NS 31 (1980), 1-16.

[4] T. H. Howard-Hill, *Ralph Crane and Some Shakespeare First Folio Comedies* (Charlottesville, Virginia, 1972), pp. 108, 113; W. W. Greg, *The Shakespeare First Folio*, p. 420.

[5] Howard-Hill, p. 123.

the play before Shakespeare handed it over to the company, the other printed from this version after it had been annotated, more or less thoroughly, by comparison with a prompt-book, with a variety of modifications deriving from the theatre. This is a difficult category, because it faces the editor with a need to make a choice, not between good and bad, but between one kind of authority and another.

A straightforward example may be cited from *A Midsummer Night's Dream*. The quarto of 1600 is generally agreed to have been printed from Shakespeare's manuscript. In the last act, Theseus is given a speech in which he both names and comments upon the entertainments offered for his wedding celebrations:

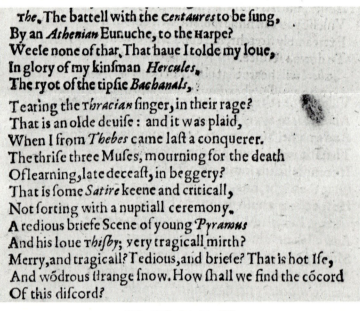

The. The battell with the *centaures* to be fung,
By an *Athenian* Eunuche, to the Harpe?
Weele none of that, That haue I tolde my loue,
In glory of my kinfman *Hercules*,
The ryot of the tipfie *Bachanals*,
Tearing the *Thracian* finger, in their rage?
That is an olde deuife : and it was plaid,
When I from *Thebes* came laft a conquerer.
The thrife three Mufes, mourning for the death
Oflearning, late deceaft, in beggery?
That is fome *Satire* keene and criticall,
Not forting with a nuptiall ceremony.
A tedious briefe Scene of young *Pyramus*
And his loue *Thifby*; very tragicall mirth?
Merry, and tragicall? Tedious, and briefe? That is hot Ife,
And wôdrous ftrange fnow. How fhall we find the côcord
Of this difcord?

(G3–G3ᵛ; 5.1.44–60)

When the play came to be printed in the First Folio (1623), a reprint of the Quarto was annotated by comparison with the theatre's prompt-book, with the result that the lines directed to be spoken by Theseus in the Quarto are now divided between him and Lysander:

Lif. The battell with the Centaurs to be fung
By an Athenian Eunuch, to the Harpe.

The. Wee'l none of that. That haue I told my Loue
In glory of my kinfman Hercules.

Lif. The riot of the tlpfie Bachanals,
Tearing the Thracian finger,in their rage?

The. That is an old deuice, and it was plaid
When I from *Thebes* came laft a Conqueror.

Lif. The thrice three Mufes,mourning for the death
of learning, late deceaft in beggerie.

The. That is fome Satire keene and criticall,
Not forting with a nuptiall ceremonie.

Lif. A tedious breefe Scene of yong *Piramus*,
And his loue *Thisby*; very tragicall mirth.

The. Merry and tragicall? Tedious,and briefe? That
is,hot ice, and wondrous ftrange fnow. How fhall wee
finde the concord of this difcord?

(O2; 5.1.44-60)

One can well imagine that when the play was put into rehearsal, either
the actor playing Theseus found difficulty in producing the vocal
variety necessary to distinguish between the titles and his comments on
them, or a member of the company—such as Shakespeare—thought that
the lines would in any case come more effectively from two speakers
than from one. An editor must choose whether to print the passage as
it stood in Shakespeare's manuscript before it was put into rehearsal,
or to print it as it was acted by Shakespeare's company.

The situation is additionally complicated by the existence of re-
ported versions of certain plays, inauthentic in themselves, inferior
in most respects to other extant editions, but containing evidence not
elsewhere available of how they were performed in Shakespeare's time,
and possibly by his company. Thus, though few texts are worse than
the first, 'bad' quarto of *Hamlet* (1603), it is the only one to tell us
that in the closet scene, the Ghost enters 'in his night gowne', or to
instruct the mad Ophelia to enter 'playing on a lute, and her haire
downe singing'. Such evidence is too precious to waste, but some

editors feel scruples about incorporating into a text directions which do not necessarily represent Shakespeare's personal intentions.

The view of the situation that I have just presented is highly summary, but it is enough, I hope, to convey some idea of the scope of the editor's problem, and also to suggest, perhaps, that the problems are more acute for one who is supervising an edition of the complete works, in which some degree of consistency of approach may seem desirable, than for the editor of a single play. The editor of a collective edition is faced with a substantial body of indispensable material, some of it written by Shakespeare, some of it not. Some of what Shakespeare wrote is self-evidently wrong, in that it contradicts manifestly superior information deriving from the text itself: I am thinking of directions such as one in the quarto of *Much Ado About Nothing* which reads '*Enter the Prince, Hero, Leonato, Iohn and Borachio, and Conrade*' (2.1.186), a direction which seems almost completely at odds with the action, since, of the characters named in it, only Don Pedro takes part in the ensuing dialogue with Benedick, who is already on stage. It is corrected in the Folio, probably on the basis of a prompt-book, to '*Enter the Prince*'. Some of the information is probably, but not certainly, wrong: I think, for instance, of directions for the entry of characters such as Hero's mother, Innogen, in *Much Ado*, or 'Beaumont' in Act Four, Scene Two of *Henry V*, or Lamprius, Rannius, Lucillius, and Mardian in Act One, Scene Two of *Antony and Cleopatra*—characters who say nothing, are not addressed, and play no part in the action, whose names Shakespeare would probably have deleted in revising his manuscript, and who probably did not appear in the play as produced, but whom nevertheless he could conceivably have wished to be present, even if in unidentifiable embodiment and only to dress the stage. Some of the information was added after Shakespeare's major act of composition was completed; it may have had his sanction, it is probably not in his words. Sometimes it undoubtedly represents contemporary theatrical practice but could conceivably represent what happened in the theatre at the suggestion of someone other than Shakespeare—in that case (if we could prove that to be the case) would it be proper to print it as Shakespeare's? Or it could even represent action added against Shakespeare's wishes, in which case we should almost certainly not wish to print it as Shakespeare's; but I can think of no certainly identifiable instance. For every play, the information that we have is in some respects inadequate, even when judged by what I take to be the most limited criterion of adequacy required in a dramatic text, that is, indication of when characters should come on the stage, and when they should leave it. And almost always, within each single text (let alone from one play to another) the information is inconsistent in its style of presentation—for example, characters are frequently designated in a variety of ways (thus, in the quarto entry directions of *Love's Labour's Lost* Costard is sometimes 'Costard', sometimes 'Clowne'; Dull is both 'Dull' and 'Constable'; Armado is sometimes 'Braggart'; and Jaquenetta is also 'Maide' and 'Wench')—and in its provision of detail.

Faced with this situation, what is an editor to do? The only easy answer is, 'prepare a diplomatic edition'—one, that is, which makes only minimal corrections of errors and anomalies in the text as originally printed. It would be perfectly possible to edit, for example, the quarto text of *Much Ado About Nothing*, or the Folio text of *All's Well that Ends Well*, as a document in its own right, perhaps with the particular aim of 'recovering' the underlying foul-paper copy. Such an endeavour would be not just legitimate, but valuable; in a sense, any serious editor undertakes it as a stage on his journey to a different end, but an undeflecting attempt to do nothing but this might yield its own rewards.

Diplomatic editions, however, are for the few. Even early compositors sometimes took the initiative in adding basic stage directions when setting from printed copy, and ever since Shakespeare's plays were first submitted to the editorial process it has been accepted that the editor of a critical edition has a responsibility to amplify the directions of his original texts. The process came naturally enough to Shakespeare's first named editor, the practising playwright Nicholas Rowe, who (in 1709) laid the foundations of modern texts; and every editor since Rowe's time who has claimed to be doing anything more than supervising the preparation of a diplomatic reprint or of a typographical or photographic facsimile has, however conservative he may have been in his treatment of dialogue, been willing to add directions which have no claim to explicit authenticity, and to adjust the original directions in the interests of clarity and consistency of presentation.

The principle behind this is enunciated by R. B. McKerrow, in his *Prolegomena for the Oxford Shakespeare* of 1939, when he formulates a distinction 'between the actual text of the plays, in the sense of the matter which is intended to be spoken by the characters, and such accessories as act and scene headings, the speakers' names, and to some extent also the stage directions, for so far at least as the *form* of these accessories is concerned there is clear evidence that in some cases this was due to the printers.' In such 'accessories', says McKerrow, 'normalization is allowable' (pp. 19-20). This is a characteristically cautious statement. Later in the *Prolegomena* McKerrow says more about each of the three categories of accessories that he distinguishes here. His remarks on act and scene divisions boil down to the view that they are, in modern editions, a necessary evil. Agreement with this view is reflected in the lack of prominence given to the divisions in, for instance, Dover Wilson's Cambridge edition, the Pelican edition, and the New Penguin Shakespeare, as opposed to, for example, the Signet and the Arden (both of which begin a new act on a fresh page with a prominent heading). On the whole, I agree with McKerrow; for most of Shakespeare's plays the Oxford edition will record the normal divisions with a few rethinkings of scene breaks, in a typographically unobtrusive manner designed to make it easy to read the plays without unwarranted interruptions. However, original research undertaken by Gary Taylor as part of the foundation for the Oxford edition shows, we believe, that from about the time that the King's Men started to use the Blackfriars Theatre in 1609-10, act intervals came normally to be marked by breaks in performance, so the divisions will be more prominently marked in texts which appear to be influenced by this practice.

On 'speakers' names', or speech prefixes, we have to agree that though they can be very revealing about Shakespeare's imaginative processes—another factor which would make a diplomatic edition valuable for specialist readers—nevertheless 'To follow the original texts in [their] irregularity would ... be unnecessarily confusing', so it is better to 'treat them as labels and to make the labels uniform' (p. 57). Again, however, we shall not accept the traditional labels unthinkingly. For example, McKerrow proposes that a character would have the same label 'throughout the play, except when a change of rank or title necessitates alteration'. In the final scene of *Love's Labour's Lost*, news is brought to the Princess of France that her father, the King, has died. The next time the King of Navarre addresses her, it is as a queen: 'How fares your Maiestie?' In the foul-paper First Quarto, 'Queen' frequently alternates with 'Princess' as a prefix for this character throughout the play; editors regularize to 'Princess' throughout, but as it seems clear that she becomes queen on her father's death, it seems to me to be as proper to alter the prefix for her remaining speeches as, in *Richard II*, to call Bolingbroke 'King Henry' after his accession, a change normally made by editors (following the First Quarto, in which however it occurs at a later point in the action than in edited texts). So 'Queen' the Princess will become in the Oxford edition.

One proposed innovation in speech prefixes in which McKerrow took pride was his plan to indicate disguise names in the prefixes. He writes:

> In several plays certain of the characters are disguised, and are addressed and referred to by other names than their own. Thus, in *The Taming of the Shrew*, Hortensio feigns to be a music-master and takes the name 'Licio', while Lucentio masquerades as 'Cambio' and Tranio as Lucentio ... On the stage there is, as a rule, little or no difficulty in penetrating the disguises and following the plot, but to a reader they may be exceedingly troublesome.
>
> I have therefore adopted the device of giving *both* the character's real name and the feigned one; the *real* name, which is the one normally used in modern editions, standing first, while the one which does not appear in the copy-text is within round brackets. Thus the prefix *Hor.* (*Lic.*) means 'Hortensio disguised as Licio' and implies that in the copy-text the name of the character is given as Hortensio. Had the disguise name been used, as was sometimes done, but not in this particular case, the speech-heading would have had the form (*Hor.*) *Lic.* (p. 58).

I have two comments on this. First, although McKerrow's system shows the best of intentions, it is rather clumsy and potentially confusing in its form, so I shall be content to add a reminder of the character's disguise, in the form '*Enter Hortensio as Licio* . . .', in the entry direction, without repeating it for every speech.

Secondly, I regard the use of abbreviated names as speech prefixes as an indefensible barbarism in anything other than a diplomatic edition. It results from the lazy-minded following of an ancient printing device presumably designed merely to save space, but perhaps resulting, too, from the blind copying by a compositor of abbreviations natural enough in an author's manuscript. It has met with some resistance; for instance, although it was followed in early volumes of the Revels plays, not all editors in the series have followed it, and some Shakespeare editions, such as the Pelican, the New Penguin, and Bevington, avoid it; but it is dying hard, and still disfigures the pages of, for instance, the Riverside and the Arden editions. Its survival, especially in one-volume editions, where space is at a premium, is helped by the fact that a lengthy prefix (Artemidorus, for example) followed by a blank verse line is apt to be too long to be fitted into the width of the average-sized page or column. But it can be avoided by printing the name above the speech in verse. The system is not always easy to operate, because it requires the editor to decide what is verse and what is prose; this is often problematical, and when the speech-prefix is printed on the same line as both verse and prose—as in the Arden edition—the distinction need not be made. But it seems proper that editors should put their minds to such matters.

On the content of stage directions, McKerrow has little to say. He notes (p. 53) that 'various editors have added a large number of stage directions', and he goes so far as to admit that not only these but 'even more elaborate ones than are usually given . . . are doubtless useful in modernized editions for the general reader'. He may sound patronizing in continuing that 'They [that is, the added directions] may often assist persons lacking in visual imagination and enable them to follow the action more easily', but he is less so in his more general discussion, where he writes (p. 1) that, for 'The great majority of those adults who now read Shakespeare', the '"best" text . . . is likely to be one completely modernized both in spelling and punctuation, with full stage directions aiding them to visualize the action as it would be if staged by a reasonably conservative producer.'

This seems a sensible enough ideal, though I should say myself that, once the decision has been made to pass beyond 'diplomatic' editing and to alter and add directions, there is no reason to make any distinction between the needs of a general reader and those of a specialist. I can conceive that bibliographers, textual critics, even literary critics may be no less lacking in the visual imagination required to infer action from dialogue than solicitors, teachers, nurses, architects, or any other representatives of 'the general reader'. Again, to be fair to McKerrow we must remember the context in which he was working. The *Prolegomena* appeared in 1939. In the same year Dover Wilson published his edition of *Richard II*, with, as its first words: '[1.1.] *A great scaffold within the castle at Windsor, with seats thereon, and a space of ground before it.*' During the 'lists' scene (1.3), one of the directions added by Wilson reads:

The trumpets sound a long flourish, as the KING and his council retire to a room at the back of the platform; the combatants remove their helmets and return to their chairs, and the spectators murmur in astonishment. After some moments, the KING returns and summons the combatants to him.

This in no way approaches Wilson's worst excesses in the directions of plays published earlier in his edition. At the end of the trial in *The Merchant of Venice*, '*Shylock totters out amid cries of execration*'. In the same play, the cue for Lorenzo's 'Come, ho, and wake Diana with a hymn' (5.1.66) reads: '*Musicians steal from the house and bestow themselves among the trees; they leave the door open behind them, and a light shines therefrom.*' And in *Julius Caesar*, the added direction (based on North's Plutarch) for Caesar's assassination reads: '*Caesar rises, and struggles to escape; the conspirators close in upon him near Pompey's statue, and hack eagerly at him; he stands awhile at bay, until, seeing Brutus about to strike also, he covers his face.*'

In this context it is understandable that McKerrow should not wish to add too much, and liberal-minded of him to allow the potential usefulness of 'even more elaborate [directions] than are usually given'. The trouble with Wilson's directions is that, at their worst, they are too wordy in expression, too emotive, and either completely non-theatrical, directing the reader's responses in the manner of a novelist— '*the KING and his council retire to a room at the back of the platform*'; or, in *A Midsummer Night's Dream* (2.2), '*The air is heavy with the scent of blossom*'—or too much tied to a particular mode of production, so that, for example, in *The Merchant of Venice* (4.1) the Duke enters amid '*a concourse of people*' attended by '*six Magnificoes in red*' (Wilson actually admits that the Magnificoes derive from Charles Kean, who, in his production at the Princess's Theatre, London, in 1858, 'arranged this scene with a Doge, attended by six senators in red, his authority being a picture at Hampton Court representing the state reception by the Doge of Sir Henry Wotton, ambassador of James I').

It is easy to mock some features of Wilson's directions. McKerrow himself writes tolerantly about them, mentioning them only in relation to the problem of collating them: 'Professor Wilson envisages the modern theatre with all its scenic resources, and supposes climbable trees, lanes, lofty turrets, and the like. Such "scenery" is perhaps not out of place in a modernized text for a modern reader, inasmuch as it may represent what was in Shakespeare's mind as he wrote and what he would have wished for in the way of setting if this had been practicable in his day. It is, however, quite impossible to record elaborations such as these without rendering the collations exceedingly long and complicated . . .' (p. 97). One sympathizes with McKerrow while acknowledging that Wilson's policy is commendable in so far as it represents a genuinely fresh attempt to solve the problem. If only Wilson had not gone as far as he did, subsequent editors might have been more willing to learn from him. I see no reason to object to his recasting of directions into a literate form, to his use of English expressions instead of *Exit* and *Exeunt*; and I positively admire some of his attempts to indicate action, costume, properties, and so on. He goes further than is necessary, and it is this that later editors have reacted against, and which has caused his edition to date rather rapidly.

Since McKerrow's work, there has been comparatively little discussion of the problem, with the exception of a valuable and stimulating article by E. A. J. Honigmann to which I shall refer again later. Greg evinces no real interest in this side of the editor's work. In *The Editorial Problem*, he confines his attention largely to the nature of the printer's copy, and the problem of the relationship between quarto and Folio texts. His aim is always to get as close to the author's manuscript as possible, and as a result he is very reluctant to admit the value of evidence derived from a prompt-book, let alone to consider adding material for which there is no verbal authority. Only if 'the reading of the promptbook was manifestly an afterthought of the author' may it be preferred to a version 'set up from the author's own manuscript' (pp. xliii–xliv): though in a footnote he adds 'Perhaps we should make a further exception in favour of stage directions required to make clear the original action. The autograph might be deficient in these.' Greg must have fully recognized that every early printing of a Shakespeare play is deficient in this way, and that most of them are seriously so; clearly he did not wish to face this particular editorial problem. Bowers has been more willing than Greg to think about the problems of a modernizing editor, but writes nothing about stage directions even in his lecture on 'Today's Shakespeare Texts, and Tomorrow's'.[6] So it seems worth taking a fresh look at the topic, starting from the basic premise that the editor needs to identify points at which additional directions, or changes to those of the early texts, are necessary to make the staging intelligible, and that he should make the additions and changes irrespective of what earlier editors have done. Of course, he can and must learn from earlier editions, but he should not—as editors have tended to do—feel that it is right to indicate necessary action when eighteenth-century editors such as Rowe, or Theobald, or Capell did so, but indelicate to do so when they did not. Nor should we accept their decisions unquestioningly. Why should our judgement be any less

---

[6] *On Editing Shakespeare*, pp. 137–79; the lecture is there reprinted from *Studies in Bibliography* 19 (1966).

good than theirs? If we stick to essentials, we shall avoid the excessive subjectivity of Dover Wilson. Of course, this does not mean that judgement will not have to be exercised. Many problems will arise, both in interpreting the evidence and in deciding what to signal.

I have been dealing so far in generalities; let me now move to an attempt to identify some of the essentials, and to indicate some specific problems.

I take it as axiomatic that the plays take place, not on heaths, in forests, in castles, in palaces, in ante-rooms, or bedrooms, or throne-rooms, but on a stage. Critics have told us so often enough, and in the past half-century editors have been showing signs of having been persuaded of the truth of this. McKerrow stated his principle plainly enough.

Some consider, and I believe rightly, that all that is necessary for the appreciation of the play is to be gathered from the text itself and that the assumption of localities not so indicated—especially when these are merely inferred from the sources or from other outside information—is undesirable. In any case indications of locality are not ordinarily to be found in the early editions. I have therefore thought it best to omit indications of locality altogether from the scene-headings of the plays, where they are usually placed (p. 60).

McKerrow's case is based mainly on authenticity. To it we must add the increasing acknowledgement in recent years that neutrality of setting is something on which Shakespeare actively plays, that there are points at which he invites us to be conscious that we are in a theatre. Nevertheless, the abandonment of indications of locality within the texts has been a slow process. They are present in all the Cambridge editions, even those prepared by J. C. Maxwell and Alice Walker. They are still to be found in Arden editions at least as late as 1965 (in J. W. Lever's *Measure for Measure*; some earlier editions in the series, such as J. P. Pafford's *Winter's Tale* (1963), had dropped them). Among editions of the complete works, Alexander's has them, so does Sisson's, so does the Signet. They are abandoned in Pelican, New Penguin, Riverside, and David Bevington's 1980 edition. They will not figure in the Oxford Shakespeare. Nevertheless, though McKerrow may be right in claiming that 'all that is necessary for the appreciation of the play is to be gathered from the text itself', such information is not always immediately apparent, so in the *Complete Oxford Shakespeare* our notes will record basically where the action takes place when this is identifiable, not in order to help readers to 'visualize the action', but to assist them in following the story.

Needless to say, and as McKerrow recognized in writing of directions that would help readers 'to visualize the action *as it would be if staged by a reasonably conservative producer*', the editor has to think in terms of the Elizabethan stage. No serious editor, I suppose, would disagree with this;[7] but it is not always easy. It is clear, for example, that, in the first scene of *Titus Andronicus*, there must be something to represent the 'tomb' in which several bodies are buried; it might be a structure brought on to the stage and taken off it; it might involve the use of one of the stage doors; it might be a trap; no one knows what Shakespeare intended, or whether, indeed, he had anything particular in mind; he might have been content to leave the problem to his company: and, of course, they may have solved it in different ways according to the different locations in which they played.[8] So it is only proper for the editor to be unspecific, though one would hope that, if space permits, he would discuss the problem and state the alternatives.

Or take an episode in *King John* (4.1) in which Hubert instructs the Executioners to 'stand | Within the arras'. The Folio—the only early text—has no direction for them either to do so, or to 'come forth' when Hubert calls them. An arras seems to have been a standard feature of the Globe[9] and of other Elizabethan theatres (E. K. Chambers, *Elizabethan Stage*, iii. 80 etc.), so probably Shakespeare has in mind the stage as much as the fiction. In this case, Dover Wilson's '*the Executioners stand behind the arras*' is acceptable. It is also conceivable (granted that plays were not always given in regular theatre buildings) that the Executioners went out of a stage door, or even that they lurked behind a pillar (such as might be found in a great hall as well as in a theatre) in a manner indicating that they were supposed to be

[7] Even so, editions in a different style may legitimately be prepared with different purposes in mind. For example, French's Acting Edition of *A Midsummer Night's Dream* (not dated, but on sale during the 1960s) offers elaborately detailed instructions, with drawings and plans, for performance in a picturesquely pictorial style: thus, the first scene is located in '*Athens. The palace of Theseus*', and '*consists of a front cloth and a dais in the C[entre], with a stone seat. No. 1 batten and floats, amber circuits, full*'. And the same play has been presented in an edition intended to facilitate a reconstruction of Peter Brook's 1970 Royal Shakespeare Company production. Needless to say, such versions extend the meaning of the word 'edition' beyond that normally understood in textual studies.

[8] There is a discussion by G. Harold Metz in 'The Early Staging of *Titus Andronicus*' (*Shakespeare Studies* 14 (1981), 99–109), pp. 104–5, though he does not consider the possible use of a trap.

[9] Bernard Beckerman, *Shakespeare at the Globe 1599-1609* (New York, 1962), p. 88.

out of sight of Hubert and Arthur. The traditional direction, Capell's *'Exeunt'*, suggests the former of these alternatives; but for an editor unwilling to commit himself to the arras, something less drastic, such as new Arden's and New Penguin's *'The Executioners withdraw'*, or Signet's *'EXECUTIONERS hide'*, seems more appropriate. (Bevington has *'The Executions go to do as they are bid'*, which shows that the problem has been recognized but seems a rather evasive way of handling it.)

There are two categories of direction which, I suppose, everyone would agree are necessary. They are entrances and exits. Characters must be got on to the stage, and off it. Even so, there are problems. I have already mentioned 'ghost' characters; some are more substantial than others. The most famous is 'Innogen', mother of Hero, the heroine of *Much Ado About Nothing*. There she is, in the play's open-ing direction: *'Enter Leonato gouernour of Messina, Innogen his wife, Hero his daughter'*, and again at the opening of the second act: *'Enter Leonato, his brother, his wife . . .'*. This is a foul-papers text; who can dispute that as he began to write each of these scenes, Shakespeare intended her to be present? Yet she says nothing, and no one either addresses her or in any other way shows awareness of her. Theobald left her out; so I believe has every subsequent editor. But another ghost has been more resistant to editorial exorcism. The Act Two direction whose opening I have just quoted continues '. . . *Hero his daughter, and Beatrice his neece, and a kinsman.'* If Innogen is a ghost, the kinsman is the shade of a shade. Rowe, who retained Innogen, dropped the kinsman. Capell substitutes the phrase *'and others'*, and seems to have been followed in this regularly for about a century and sporadically thereafter (for example by Alexander). The kinsman is not in the (old) Cambridge edition, or the Oxford; he is in the New Variorum (1899)—understandably, since this is a reprint of the Folio text—and after this he materializes frequently. He has been the subject of some biographical speculation: Dover Wilson thought he might be 'the mute son' of Antonio (deaf as well, perhaps); Grace Trenery, in her (old) Arden edition, is followed by Arthur Humphreys, in his new Arden edition, in making the same conjecture, because earlier, Antonio is asked where his son is (1.2.1). Chambers went further: 'Much of the stage-direction and speech-prefix confusion can be cleared up by realizing that the singer Balthaser is also Anthonio's son and Leonato's "cousin" and "kinsman"' (p. 386)—fictions which well exemplify that 'irritable reaching after fact and reason' which goes along with the determination to believe that Shakespeare had worked out every last detail of his plot.

Perhaps the kinsman's very nebulousness has helped to keep him on the page if not on the boards: as the Cambridge editors delicately put it, 'It is impossible to conceive that Hero's mother should have been present during the scenes in which the happiness and honour of her daughter were at issue, without taking a part, or being once referred to.' (In other words, she couldn't have kept her mouth shut.) A mere kinsman may be thought more capable of being silent though present. Possibly those editors who have retained him have regarded him as an attendant. But there is no evidence elsewhere that Leonato would normally be attended; the kinsman would be a considerable embarrassment on stage during this long scene; and the fact that he is given a slightly less neutral status than that of an attendant suggests that Shakespeare did originally intend to involve him in the action. His case seems exactly parallel to that of Innogen; all editors exorcise her, and in all logic they should have laid him to rest, too.

Not only ghost characters cause problems in entries. I have discussed elsewhere, for example, a number of places in *Much Ado About Nothing* where Shakespeare seems to have been hazy about the point at which characters should enter. Further investigations into these and similar matters will not necessarily result in certainty, but they should encourage us to look at earlier editorial decisions for what they are, to question them, to admit uncertainty when our editorial procedure and apparatus permit us to do so, and to see the play texts as more flexible, more open to legitimate variation of interpretation, than they may previously have seemed. It is, for example, often desirable to question editorial provision of non-speaking attendants, especially in scenes involving high-ranking persons. McKerrow, remarking that editors 'have frequently added "Attendants", "Courtiers", "Soldiers", etc. when the early texts simply mark the entrance of the principal persons', states that his 'practice has been only to add names of persons who actually *speak* or are individually addressed when these happen to be omitted. It may, of course, as a general rule be taken for granted that a King does not appear in state without being accompanied by a certain number of attendants . . .' (p. 54). This is fair, but it is not always easy to determine whether or not a king is 'in state'. At the opening of Act One, Scene Two of *The Winter's Tale*, for instance, where the Folio direction reads '*Enter Leontes, Hermione, Mamillius, Polixenes, Camillo*', Theobald added '*and attendants*', and is followed in this by most, if not all, recent editors. They may be right; two kings, a queen, and a prince are on stage; but this is not a state occasion; modern directors often present the scene as a domestic one, and as the only early text permits this, I see no reason to add to its direction.

At other times, clarification of entries seems desirable. A scene which is, I think, badly served by modern editors is Act Three, Scene One of *Julius Caesar*—the scene of Caesar's murder. Here I will mention only the opening entry. The Folio has a mass entry: *Flourish. Enter Caesar, Brutus, Cassius, Caska, Decius, Metellus, Trebonius, Cynna, Antony, Lepidus, Artimedorus, Publius, and the Soothsayer*: an awful lot of people, you would think, to troop on to the stage through one door, especially as you need to add Popilius to it, since he speaks early in the scene. The opening dialogue is

> *Caes⟨ar⟩.* The Ides of March are come.
> *Sooth⟨sayer⟩.* I *Caesar*, but not gone.
> *Art⟨emidorus⟩.* Haile *Caesar*: Read this Scedule.

Can we really believe that all the characters should come on one after another before any of them speaks? Is it not far more likely that Artemidorus and the Soothsayer should enter by a different door from the rest? And if so, should an editor not say so? Earlier editors showed some sense of this. Capell directs that the Senate is sitting: '*In the Entrance, and amid a Throng of People*, ARTEMIDORUS, *and the* Soothsayer. *Flourish, and Enter* CAESAR, *attended*', and so on. The opening part of this is questionable, but it shows some sense of the stage—even if not of Shakespeare's stage—and also a sense of responsibility to both author and reader. Capell's direction is followed by many later editors, reaching its apogee in Dover Wilson's characteristic elaboration (1949):

> *Before the Senate House; Senators in session seen through open doors, with an empty chair of gold at the head of their table; without, a statue of Pompey beside one of the doors.*
> *A crowd of people stand waiting; among them* ARTEMIDORUS *and the Soothsayer . . .*

More recent editors shy away from this. I think they are right to do so, but not to retreat back to the unadulterated Folio version, as, for instance, the Arden, the New Penguin, the Riverside, and even Bevington do.

Sometimes, too, an original entry direction is open to variety of interpretation about who exactly is supposed to enter. So at the beginning of the episode of the masque (1.5) of *Romeo and Juliet*, the good quarto (a foul-papers text) has the direction *'Enter all the guests and gentlewomen to the Maskers'*. This must include Lady Capulet, but does it also include the Nurse? The new Arden editor follows usual practice in bringing the Nurse on at this point, but she is certainly not a guest and scarcely, I should have thought, a gentlewoman. She is not demonstrably needed until late in the scene, after Romeo and Juliet have spoken their love-sonnet, and kissed. Then the Nurse says 'Madam your mother craues a word with you.' If Lady Capulet is on state, why does she speak through the Nurse? Reasons might be suggested. But Shakespeare sometimes omits necessary entrances and exits. And he had problems with the unavoidable complexities of ballroom scenes (there is another tricky one in *Much Ado About Nothing*). It would be proper for an editor at least to suggest the possibility that Shakespeare either imagined Lady Capulet to have left the stage, or forgot that she was still on, and that he intended the Nurse to make her entrance with her message. (This would, incidentally, reinforce the Arden editor's admirable perception, made in his note to 2.2.149, that the Nurse's repeated interruptions form 'a kind of miniature conceit for the tragic action as a whole'.)

If characters have to get on the stage, they must also get off. Early editions frequently omit to indicate when they should do so. Editors, too, occasionally fail to do so. (This may, incidentally, be a sign of virtue; editors marking paste-ups from earlier editions, or typing from them, are likely to benefit from centuries of editorial practice; those working directly from early editions are at greater risk. Perhaps this is the misfortune suffered by Alfred Harbage in the Pelican *Love's Labour's Lost*, Act Four, Scene One, where he provides no exit for Katherine.) There is also the danger of marking exits at the wrong place.

There is a probable instance in Act Two, Scene Four of *The Two Gentlemen of Verona*. The servant, Speed, speaks three times in the first seven lines, then not at all for the more than two hundred lines of the scene that remain. The Cambridge editors instructed him to depart after his last speech. Theatrically, this may seem better than leaving him standing around like the proverbial spare dinner. Yet, as Valentine's page, he could remain in silent attendance. Clifford Leech—the new Arden editor—noting the Cambridge editors' remark that '"the clown" would not be kept as a mute bystander', says 'But Speed is a page, not a clown'. This does not, perhaps, settle the issue as authoritatively as the terseness of the phrasing implies; probably

Shakespeare simply forgot about Speed as the scene developed, and it seems right to draw attention, without dogmatism, to the alternative possibilities.

If entries and exits are essentials, there are many other types of direction which editors have been inclined to add, but have tended to do so inconsistently. These too need to be rethought. I think of directions for action such as fighting, beating, kneeling, standing, kissing, and so on; of whether speeches should be spoken aside; of whether we should name the person addressed; of the indicating of special costumes or properties. In these matters, we come up against the problem of editorial tact. It is often suggested that there is no need to add directions for action which is evident from the text. Up to a point, this is acceptable. I should not insist, for instance, that after the Prince of Morocco says 'Let's see—what says this leaden casket?', the editor should add *'He looks at the leaden casket'*. But I am prepared more often than many previous editors have been to offer help to readers even at the risk of appearing to insult their intelligence. After all, there are times when action seems to be implied by the text but certainly should not happen. For instance, in Act Four, Scene Three of *The Comedy of Errors* Dromio of Syracuse rushes in to Antipholus of Syracuse with the words 'Master, here's the gold you sent me for.' A reader might reasonably infer that Dromio should hand the gold over, but some twenty-five lines later Dromio says again 'Here are the angels that you sent for . . .', so it seems likely that he should not have handed them over earlier. If a reader has been trained, as it were, to believe that action apparently implied by the text should take place whether or not it is marked by a direction, he is likely to be misled here.

Some problems arise from inconsistencies in early editions, and, indeed, in the author's own practice. So in *Timon of Athens*, printed in the Folio, we have the speech

> Ha: is not that his Steward muffled so?   (3.4.40; TLN 1169)

It is perfectly obvious from this line that Flavius should be muffled; an editor who inserted the instruction that he should be so would be liable to accusations of officiousness. But the Folio stage direction preceding this line is *'Enter Steward in a Cloake, muffled'*, so all editors retain the instruction. In *Troilus and Cressida*, however, when Pandarus brings Cressida to Troilus (3.2.38), the direction in both quarto and Folio merely names the characters entering; Pandarus speaks some eight or more sentences before there is any clue to the reader that

Cressida, too, is 'muffled': 'Come draw this curtaine, and lets see your picture.' No editor, I suppose, doubts that the *curtain* before the *picture* is the *veil* before the face that it explicitly is in *Twelfth Night*: 'Giue me my vaile ... we will draw the Curtain, and shew you the picture', says Olivia (1.5.156, 217-18; TLN 459, 524). Yet, to the best of my belief, it was not until David Bevington's edition of 1980 that any editor provided this information in the entry direction: *Enter Pandarus and Cressida, [veiled]*. It seems to me *more* of an insult to a reader to suppose that he does not care about information essential to an intelligent reading of the play than to omit to provide such information just because it is not provided in an early edition, however inconsistent the directions of that edition may be either within itself or in relation to other plays. It is true that the reader may deduce this information; but the spectator has it presented to him immediately upon Cressida's entrance, whereas the reader who *does* deduce it then has to read it back, as it were, into the earlier part of the scene, so that failure to provide the information is a potential stumbling-block.

The principle operative here is a theatrical one: that the editor may sometimes be able to provide information at a point equivalent to that at which its visual correlative would be apprehended in the theatre. So, for example, it seems useful at the opening of Act Three, Scene Three of *The Winter's Tale*, when Antigonus comes in carrying the baby Perdita, to mention too that Antigonus is carrying a box (or bundle) and a scroll; and to add, when Autolycus says 'Let me pocket up my pedlar's excrement', the information that he takes off his false beard (4.4.702), and to indicate, when the Old Shepherd and his son make their entrance at court, that they are dressed as gentlemen (5.2.119). I think, too, that it is often important for a reader that the editor should indicate to whom speeches, or parts of speeches, are addressed; the basis on which I work is that I consider adding such information whenever a speech is clearly *not* addressed to the previous speaker. It is desirable, too, to indicate when one group of characters moves out of earshot of another, when speeches are given aside, and even sometimes when they are addressed to the audience.

I should say that, although I am more willing to add directions than many editors, I do not think I differ much from predecessors and colleagues in the *kinds* of direction I would add. I am seeking improvements in consistency; I am suggesting that we should be rather bolder than most of us have been about acting on our own judgement, without requiring editorial precedent. But few, if any, of the new directions in the *Complete Oxford Shakespeare* will be different in kind from those to which readers of scholarly editions are accustomed. It may even be that some traditional directions will be dropped.

Take, for example, a point in the episode of the Clown who brings the asps to Cleopatra in the last scene of *Antony and Cleopatra*. The Folio's entry direction reads *'Enter Guardsman, and Clowne'*. After the Clown has left, and Cleopatra, Charmian, and Iras have died, Dolabella asks 'Who was last with them?' A Guard replies 'A simple Countryman, that broght hir Figs: This was his Basket.' So editors since Rowe have, quite properly, added 'with a basket', or some similar phrase, to his entry direction. During the scene Cleopatra attempts to dismiss the Clown with the words 'Get thee hence, farewell.' The Clown then says 'I wish you all ioy of the Worme', and at this point Capell added the direction *'setting down his basket'*. Capell is followed by most modern editors—Kittredge, Dover Wilson, Emrys Jones, Riverside. There is no evidence for this action; it assumes that the Clown takes Cleopatra's hint, whereas it is just as likely that he should completely fail to do so, and that this should itself be a source of comedy; the direction has been repeated by editors who would not have dreamed of adding it for themselves. Bevington, who has done more than most recent editors to rethink stage directions, drops it— quite rightly, I think, though he might have gone a little further and added 'leaving the basket' to the Clown's exit direction.

We are increasingly coming to see, too, that 'asides' have been too liberally marked—the subject is well treated by E. A. J. Honigmann in his article 'Re-enter the Stage Direction'.[10] Nor do I propose to be other than businesslike in the wording of directions. This is sometimes a problem: again, tact is required. In plays for which the early directions are very sparse—some of those believed to have been printed from transcripts by Crane—uniformity in the style of directions is attainable, but in texts which preserve idiosyncratically Shakespearian directions, it is not. I prefer to avoid the conscious introduction of archaism: I cannot even bring myself to print *Paulina . . . discovers Hermione*, a direction added by Rowe in which *discovers*, meaning 'reveals', requires annotation for a modern student. I think that non-Shakespearian additions in a scholarly edition should be in language which does not jar with what surrounds it, but which is, so far as possible, intelligible to the modern reader. We shall translate theatre Latin which is no

[10] 'Re-enter the Stage Direction: Shakespeare and Some Contemporaries', *Shakespeare Survey 29* (Cambridge, 1976), 117–25.

longer in common use—'*solus*', '*manet*', and so on—but retain '*Exit*' and '*Exeunt*', which have, as McKerrow says, 'become more or less anglicized' (p. 53).

I qualified what I just said with the phrase 'in a scholarly edition'. Again we need to recognize that plays may properly be edited in different ways to suit different readers. I am assuming that our editions will be used mainly by students and scholars with a concern for authenticity. We shall not print square brackets to signal alterations or additions to directions when we believe that they are indisputable: when they merely regularize names, for instance, or when they indicate action which is indisputably required by the text. I find square brackets an irritating distraction, and I think that their use inhibits editors from providing necessary information. Even McKerrow, in his plans for a designedly conservative edition, clearly had reservations about their use: 'I do not defend them in the stage directions on any logical grounds. They are simply a matter of convenience. If it is understood that a bracketed name or direction is not in the copy-texts, this will in practice often save much space in the collation notes' (pp. 50-1). In our OET editions, we *shall* collate all alterations; we have less need than McKerrow for concern about space in the collation notes, as we are not attempting historical collations; so all alterations and additions will be readily identifiable on the page on which they have been made. In the complete edition we shall rely more on the reader's confidence, but the *Textual Companion* will print all the directions of the relevant early edition or editions, so again it will be possible for the interested reader to see where changes have been made.

I should like to add that I have no inherent objection to a far freer treatment of stage directions than I have suggested here. I should not always wish to go as far as Dover Wilson. I should wish that, even in an edition of Shakespeare intended simply for someone who wanted to read the plays for pleasure, with no ulterior, academic motives, the directions should bear in mind the theatre for which the plays were written. But I should have no scholarly compunctions about casting the original directions into complete sentences, about using English expressions instead of *Exit* and *Exeunt*, and about adding information derived from the text with considerably more freedom than in an edition intended mainly for students. But that is not the enterprise upon which I am engaged at present.

4

THE EDITOR AND THE THEATRE: ACT ONE OF *TITUS ANDRONICUS*

So far, I have discussed staging problems largely as if the editor's basic evidence came from a single early text, taking little account of the special problems that arise when there are two basic texts, one pre-theatrical, as it were—a quarto printed from foul papers—the other printed from a manuscript or an annotated quarto which has been influenced by theatre practice. This situation faces the editor with the need, not merely to decide how far to go in indicating the text's implied staging, but also to choose between variants. In this chapter I wish to concentrate on the first act (which forms a single, long scene) of a play—*Titus Andronicus*—which falls into this category.

The two authoritative texts are the quarto of 1594, of which the unique surviving copy is preserved in the Folger Shakespeare Library in Washington, DC, and the First Folio, set up from the second reprint (Q3, 1611) of the quarto with additional and variant stage directions, an extra line (and an extra, meaningless phrase), and a whole additional scene (the 'fly' scene, 3.2). It is generally assumed either (with Greg) that the copy of Q3 used for the Folio had been annotated for use as a prompt-book (or that it had been annotated by comparison with a copy of Q2 which had been marked in the same way,[1] or (with Dover Wilson) that the copy of Q3 had been directly annotated from a manuscript prompt-book.[2] I favour the latter hypothesis. The Quarto is, by general agreement, printed from Shakespeare's own, 'foul', papers. Its directions are, as Greg writes, 'descriptive and literary, very much what we should expect from an author not closely connected with the theatre'.[3] Clearly it must stand as our prime witness to what Shakespeare wrote. But the Folio is our only authority for a complete scene generally agreed to be by Shakespeare, and for another

---

[1] Greg, *The Editorial Problem*, p. 120.

[2] J. Dover Wilson, 'The Copy for *Titus Andronicus*', *Titus Andronicus* (Cambridge, 1948), pp. 94-7. This is also the view of E. M. Waith (*Titus Andronicus*, the Oxford Shakespeare (Oxford, 1984), pp. 40-3).

[3] *The Editorial Problem*, p. 117.

line (1.1.398) usually regarded as authentic; it also includes directions which are clearly theatrical rather than literary. If its additional dialogue is authoritative, are not the directions likely to be equally so?

The answer is 'not necessarily, quite'. They need not have emanated directly from Shakespeare; they could conceivably misrepresent his intentions. We do not know the date of the prompt copy used by the annotator (on Greg's hypothesis, it cannot have predated 1600, when Q2 was published, and may be as late as 1611, when Q3 appeared). It could represent a staging of the play later than, and different from, that which it originally received, possibly even one put on after Shakespeare had died. In all probability it would be a palimpsest, with directions for later performances added to, and in some cases substituted for, earlier ones—as in the surviving manuscripts of the anonymous plays *Edmund Ironside* and *Woodstock*, and the prompt-book (based on a printed text) of *A Looking Glass for London and England* by Robert Greene and Thomas Lodge. J. C. Maxwell, in his (original) new Arden edition of 1953, stated 'The new stage-directions are of some interest for the staging of this popular play, and reflect the increased use of music in the early seventeenth century.'[4] This appears to reflect Greg's view, based on his theory about the copy, that the Folio 'shows us the stage arrangements current at a comparatively late date'.[5] But Maxwell accepted Wilson's hypothesis rather than Greg's, and Greg, reviewing the edition, remarked 'if Mr. Maxwell had thought rather more deeply on the matter he could have hardly written' this, 'for if Q1 was printed from foul papers and the F directions added from the prompt-book, there is no reason to suppose that the latter do not go back to the original production'.[6] Maxwell concurred, in his revision of 1961. If Greg himself had thought even more deeply, it might have occurred to him that a prompt-book used for annotating a copy of either Q2 (1600) or Q3 (1611) might well have included directions from a production later than the first, especially as he appears to agree that it contained a scene of later date than the rest of the play. Still, one

---

[4] *Titus Andronicus*, ed. J. C. Maxwell, the Arden Shakespeare (London, 1953), p. xviii. The publishers regard this as a second edition, though it is in no normal sense a revision of the earlier Arden *Titus Andronicus* (ed. H. Bellyse Baildon, 1904). Maxwell's revision of 1961 is thus, technically, the third edition. Page references in this chapter are normally to the 1953 edition, but note is taken of all revisions in the 1961 version. Unless otherwise stated, passages cited are unaltered in the revision (as here).

[5] *The Editorial Problem*, p. 120.

[6] *Modern Language Review* 49 (1954), 360–4; p. 363.

cannot deny that variants deriving from a prompt-book, even of a first production, are not necessarily totally authoritative. The dilemma is expressed by Greg:

the two most important sources of the extant texts are probably the author's foul papers and theatrical prompt-books. But foul papers are often characterized by the fact that the text has not everywhere been reduced to final form: the writer knew that it had to go through a further process that might cause disturbance and would at the same time afford an opportunity for tidying up loose ends. In a properly constructed prompt-book the text no doubt received this final revision, but we can never be sure at whose hand it received it. Worse still we can never know how far merely theatrical considerations of casting, censorship, and the like, may have wrested the text from the true intention of the author.[7]

This is an overstatement, but it identifies a real dilemma. Choice is inevitable. Do we prefer the play a little undercooked, perhaps even half-baked, or do we like it in a more finished form, even if a hand other than the author's may have added some of the icing? The prompt-book must be one that was used by Shakespeare's company; the play was written to be staged; in the absence of any other evidence about its theatrical realization, it may seem prodigal to ignore that provided by the Folio. This is, however, the policy that J. C. Maxwell appears to be advocating when he writes, in the Introduction to his Arden edition,

As *Titus* is neither a play with a complicated staging nor one which will ever be widely read, I have thought it worthwhile, at the cost of a few oddities, to sweep away almost the whole paraphernalia of later editorial stage-directions and return to Q1, with only occasional supplements (p. xxiii).

That the staging of the play is not, in fact, uncomplicated I expect to demonstrate in the following pages. When Maxwell offers as justification of his policy the statement that the play will never be widely read, he implies, I suppose, that those who read it are likely to be specialists who will not need help. This would be acceptable as justification for a diplomatic edition of the Quarto, consistently offering that text, emended where necessary in its own terms, but not attempting to fill in any gaps. But this is not what Maxwell prepared; in the event, it seems to me, he fell between two stools.

[7] *The Editorial Problem*, p. 156.

As a basis for a pragmatic examination of the editor's problems in dealing with stage directions in collateral texts, and as a basis too for discussion of some possible solutions, I have chosen the first scene of *Titus Andronicus* because it offers (*pace* Maxwell) particular difficulties in understanding and visualizing the staging. It is, of course, vital that the reader should understand what is going on. This is the expository scene, and if we fail to grasp who is who and what is what at this point we shall have problems throughout the play, and our reading of it will be impaired—or uncompleted, because failure to grasp the opening situation is just the sort of thing that makes a student (or any other reader) give up in despair. I hope to suggest, too, that acknowledgement of the need to consider the requirements of the play's staging may lead to a greater understanding of the text as a whole. I shall consider the treatment of the scene in, particularly, two reputable and influential modern editions: Maxwell's Arden, which dates from 1953 with a revision in 1961, and G. Blakemore Evans's Riverside edition, of 1974.[8] I have already cited Maxwell's statement about his editorial policy. Evans merely states (p. 1051) that he is using Q1 as copy-text except for Act Three, Scene Two; on the Folio, he remarks that it 'was printed from a copy of Q3, which Greg feels may well have served as a prompt-book', offering no views on its variant directions.

The opening direction in the Quarto reads: '*Enter the* Tribunes *and* Senatours *aloft*: *And then enter* Saturninus *and his followers at one dore, and* Bassianus *and his followers, with Drums and Trumpets.*' The Folio varies this, adding an opening '*Flourish*', the phrase '*at the other*'—that is, the other door—after '*Bassianus and his followers*', and changing '*with Drums and Trumpets*' to '*Drum & Colours*'.

Let us take the first word first. '*Flourish*' says the Folio, but not the Quarto. Neither Maxwell nor Evans prints it; Maxwell collates it, Evans does not. Collation, at least, seems desirable. A preliminary flourish does not seem out of place in a play which opens as formally as this, and though here, as on many other occasions, Shakespeare apparently did not specify one in his foul papers, he may have omitted to do so only because it seemed unnecessary to specify anything so obviously appropriate. So I should throw caution to the winds, take my reputation as a scholar in both hands, and print '*Flourish*'.

---

[8] This chapter represents the thinking behind my edition of *Titus Andronicus* in the forthcoming *Complete Oxford Shakespeare*. I have benefited from correspondence with Eugene M. Waith about his edition of the play in the Oxford English Texts series, and am grateful to him for his share in the dialogue.

Now the next word: *'Enter'*, in both Quarto and Folio. Simple
enough, you might think. Yet Maxwell, while retaining it in his text,
denies it in a footnote—or says, at least, that it does not mean what it
seems to mean: 'This does not mean that we see them coming on, but
that they are "discovered" by drawing back the curtains of the upper
stage.' He supports this with G. F. Reynolds's citation of a direction
from *George a Greene* (*c*.1590), scene xi: *'Enter a Shoemaker sitting
upon the stage at worke.'* Certainly that appears to show that *'Enter'*
could mean 'There is discovered', but it is not adequate evidence that
a number of characters could be discovered *'aloft'*, as the Quarto
direction specifies, and I know of no evidence for curtains on the
'upper stage'. So I see no reason to deny the literal meaning of the
original direction.

G. K. Hunter, pointing out that Tribunes and Senators were 'traditionally hostile', has suggested that they may enter separately;[9] but
we have no evidence about Shakespeare's intentions, or about the
practice of his company, so this, I suggest, is beyond the editor's brief,
though it may well be worth a note.

Let us proceed a little further. *'Enter the* Tribunes *and* Senatours . . .'
No hope of passing rapidly on: who are the Tribunes and Senators?
Neither Quarto nor Folio, of course, gives us a cast list. Editors supply
one. The only named character described by both Maxwell and Evans
as either a tribune or a senator is Marcus Andronicus, whom both
editors list as *'tribune of the People, and brother to Titus'*. To fill the
gap implied by the direction, the editors list 'Tribunes and Senators'
among the miscellaneous characters. That is fair. The problem is Marcus
Andronicus. He is a tribune, so it might seem reasonable that Evans
names him in the opening direction: *'Enter the* TRIBUNES, [*among
them* MARCUS ANDRONICUS] *and* SENATORS *aloft . . .'*. This is
more helpful than Maxwell, who leaves it to a later note (on line 18) to
say 'Marcus has been on stage with the other Tribunes from the beginning of the scene.' But is it right? The reason for doubt originates in a
direction at line 17. *'Marcus Andronicus with the Crowne'* says the
Quarto. This is not necessarily an entry direction. It is not followed
by a speech prefix, though Marcus clearly speaks the lines that follow,
and the direction (which is centred) is usually interpreted to mean
simply that he is visibly holding the crown while he speaks. So our
editors replace the direction by a speech prefix followed by the phrase

---

[9] 'Flatcaps and Bluecoats: Visual Signals on the Elizabethan Stage', *Essays and
Studies* 33 (1980), 16–47.

'[*holding the crown*]'. This ignores the evidence of the Folio, which has the direction '*Enter Marcus Andronicus aloft with the Crowne.*' This could, admittedly, represent simply a scribe's or compositor's misguidedly helpful but unauthoritative and mistaken interpretation of the Quarto direction, though the fact that the addition is not merely of '*Enter*' but also of '*aloft*' may give us pause before we accept this explanation. The addition merely of '*Enter*' may be regarded as no more than officiousness, but the further addition of '*aloft*' looks suspiciously like carefulness. It seems to me quite plausible that Marcus, carrying the crown, should enter later than the other Tribunes.[10] After all, if he were present, carrying the crown, from the start, it would be fairly obvious that he had something to say; and if he were present but not obviously carrying the crown, then either something would have to be done to get it to him at line 17, or he would have to bring it out of concealment. In my opinion, since the Quarto direction does not deny the possibility that he first appears, 'aloft', at l. 17, and since the text influenced by the prompt-book actually says he does, the evidence supports the Folio direction, and this should be preferred (as it traditionally was until editors chose to ignore the Folio in favour of the Quarto).

We can now proceed a little more rapidly. There is not, I think, any problem with *aloft*, though Dover Wilson managed to create one. His characteristically fanciful direction begins:

> *An open place in Rome, before the Capitol, beside the entrance to which there stands the monument of the Andronici. Through a window opening on to the balcony of an upper chamber in the Capitol may be seen the Senate in session.*

Not too easily, I should have thought. This reads more like a direction for a film than for a play on the Elizabethan stage. In effect, it drops the 'Tribunes *and* Senatours', and in doing so lessens the dramatic tension that Shakespeare is at pains to create among his three groups of characters, one on the upper level and the other two on the main stage.

---

[10] On the evidence of the unpublished galley proofs of McKerrow's Oxford edition (see p. 99 below), this is how he interpreted the direction. His draft note (in typescript) reads: 'Later editors follow F1 in indicating the entry of Marcus Andronicus here. It is, however, possible that he was originally intended to enter with the Tribunes and Senators at the opening of the scene . . . [Q1's direction] may . . . have indicated nothing more than that Marcus, holding the crown, now spoke in answer to Saturninus and Bassianus. I follow F1 with doubts.' Some modern editors, for example Bevington (1980), also follow F1.

Possibly, though not certainly, the Senators are involved in the action by the first words spoken:

> Noble *Patricians*, Patrons of my Right,
> Defend the iustice of my cause with armes

begs Saturninus. He continues

> And Countrimen my louing followers,
> Plead my successiue Title with your swords . . .

It is usually assumed that all four lines are addressed to the supporters whom Saturninus has brought with him, but to me it seems possible that the first two should be addressed to the characters on the upper stage (Senators were patricians, though Tribunes were not). But this is arguable, so I do not suggest it should be reflected in the directions.

Each editor adds the Folio's phrase *'at the other [doore]'*, and there can be no dispute about this. The only remaining problem in this direction lies in the Quarto's phrase *'with Drums and Trumpets'* and the Folio's alteration of it to *'with Drum & Colours'*. First, does the phrase refer only to Bassianus and his followers, or to both groups? Presumably to both, as both are belligerent. If this is agreed, then it would be helpful of an editor to remove the ambiguity. Our editors do not. Secondly, should we follow Quarto's *'Drums and Trumpets'* or Folio's *'Drum & Colours'*? Here there is perhaps room for argument. The Quarto undoubtedly represents Shakespeare's first intentions. The Folio probably represents what happened in the theatre. Whether the singular *'Drum'* (for *'Drums'*) is significant is hard to say. Perhaps we might guess that one *'Drum'*—or drummer—accompanied each faction; or the alteration may even be accidental. *'Colours'*—meaning, I suppose, one or more standard-bearers—may have replaced *'Trumpets'* for either practical or aesthetic reasons, or both. The preliminary *'Flourish'* may have required all the available trumpeters; and to follow it with additional trumpeting may have seemed redundant. My inclination, again, would be to follow the Folio, collating the Quarto. Our editors follow the Quarto—logically, since they have also rejected the Folio's *'Flourish'*; they collate the Folio, and in this Evans seems inconsistent, as he had not recorded Folio's *'Flourish'*. He compounds his inconsistency later in the scene, at line 63, where the Folio adds a *'Flourish'* to the Quarto's direction *'They goe vp into the Senate house.'* Evans accepts the *'Flourish'* here, where Maxwell is consistent in his fidelity to the quarto. (Exactly the same happens at l. 398.)

Shortly before this, Bassianus and Saturninus have calmed down in response to Marcus' 'Let vs intreat . . . That you withdraw you, and abate your strength, | Dismisse your followers, and as suters should, | Pleade your deserts in peace and humblenes.' Each has a speech. Bassianus declares

> . . . I will here dismisse my louing friends:
> And to my fortunes and the peoples fauour,
> Commit my cause in ballance to be waid.

And Saturninus addresses his followers:

> Friends that haue beene thus forward in my right.
> I thanke you all, and here dismisse you all,
> And to the loue and fauour of my Countrie,
> Commit my selfe, my person, and the cause.

Both the Quarto and the Folio direct *'Exit Soldiers'* after the last line of Bassianus' speech; our editors follow, while also adding a similar direction for the departure of Saturninus' soldiers. This seems logical, but it leaves a problem, because, after Saturninus and Bassianus leave the stage—which then, according to our editors, is empty—a Captain has to enter calling 'Romaines make way', in the circumstances an unrealistic demand. Hunter assumes 'that the Captain here addresses the theatre audience, who at this point represent the Roman mob'.[11] This is what happened in John Barton's 1981 Royal Shakespeare Company production, and it worked well. But it may alternatively be the result of Shakespeare's carelessness in not providing for the entry at the beginning of the scene of Romans other than followers of Bassianus and Saturninus. It is the kind of problem which can be overcome at rehearsal without the provision of extra dialogue. The two most obvious solutions are to ignore—or, in effect, modify—the direction *'Exit Soldiers'*, and the implicit direction for the exit of Saturninus' 'friends', so that, perhaps, the 'followers' are 'dismissed' to the extent that they relax their bellicose postures but remain on stage, or, alternatively (as Hunter also suggests), that some leave and some remain behind. An editor may hesitate to tamper with the original directions to the extent needed to suggest either of these alternatives, but at least, in an annotated text, he could show that he recognizes the problem.

---

[11] 'Flatcaps and Bluecoats', p. 18n.

I referred to the exit of Bassianus and Saturninus. Saturninus, after dismissing his followers, says

> Rome be as iust and gratious vnto me,
> As I am confident and kinde to thee.
> Open the gates and let me in.

And Bassianus adds

> Tribunes and me a poore Competitor.

(I take it that 'competitor' means 'co-petitioner', though our editors—and most others—leave this obsolete sense unglossed.) Bassianus' word 'Tribunes' must mean that he is addressing those on the upper level, so Saturninus' 'Rome' may be taken to have the same significance, and I think it would be helpful and unexceptionable for an editor to add 'to the *Tribunes and Senators*' before Saturninus' 'Rome . . .'. No one does so. The Folio's *Flourish*, to which I referred, no doubt accompanies, or is a signal for, the opening of the 'gates'—presumably a pair of central stage doors (or, failing these, a recess). Such doors often figured in siege scenes,[12] and this scene resembles the basic theatrical 'siege' pattern, with two rival armies on the main stage and with representatives of a city aloft. After the armies are dismissed, the two leaders in such scenes are then allowed 'into the city', probably through a different door from those through which their armies have departed.

The exit direction in *Titus* for Bassianus and Saturninus is interesting: *'They goe vp into the Senate house'* (so, substantially, both Quarto and Folio). Evidently Shakespeare was thinking in terms of his fiction, not of his stage. Editors let this stand, justifiably, perhaps—certainly we should not want to lose it altogether—but not, I think, until David Bevington's 1980 edition was anyone so helpful as to add a note: 'The gates . . . are presumably a door in the façade of the tiring house, rearstage, below the gallery. Saturninus and Bassianus presumably exit through this door and ascend inside the tiring house to the gallery or Senate House, where they reappear with the Tribunes and Senators.'[13] That seems to me admirable, and in case anyone should think it is all

---

[12] See *Henry V*, ed. Gary Taylor (Oxford, 1982), second note to 3.3.80.1–2.
[13] Hunter ('Flatcaps and Bluecoats', p. 18) says that they go 'by separate doors, one must assume', but a formal departure through a central door representing the 'gates' seems equally possible. Presumably the upper level party should then 'freeze' into some kind of tableau, though Hunter says 'the people on the upper stage retire out of sight, though the understanding is that the Senate meeting is going on up there, just outside the limits of the visible' (p. 18).

too obvious, it is worth looking at the editorial history of the later part of the scene. Having brought Tribunes and Senators on to the upper level at the start of the play, and then, by implication, having sent Bassianus and Saturninus to join them, a remarkable number of editors seem to forget all about them. True, Shakespeare himself may have done so, as they are silent and uninvolved throughout the episode in which Titus inters his slaughtered sons, commands the sacrifice of his captive Tamora's son, Alarbus, and is welcomed by Lavinia.[14] But after this, in the episode starting at 1. 169, Marcus Andronicus, Bassianus, Saturninus, and the Tribunes speak. Neither Quarto nor Folio offers a direction at the point at which they rejoin the action, and this is quite understandable on the assumption that they should simply have remained silent 'aloft'. But Maxwell, astonishingly, adds the direction '*Enter* MARCUS ANDRONICUS *and Tribunes; re-enter* SATURNINUS, BASSIANUS, *and others*' even though he has not directed any of them to leave the stage. He attributes the direction, in substance, to Alexander Dyce, which is unfair to Dyce, whose actual entry reads '*Enter* below, *Marcus Andronicus*'—that is, he is instructing him to reappear after leaving the upper level, an instruction which, if mistaken, is at least more rational than an instruction for someone to enter who has not been instructed to depart. Maxwell's note (though not his direction) says that 'this entry is on the upper stage'. The Riverside editor does better in reminding his readers what the situation is:

> *Marcus Andronicus, attended by the other Tribunes, with Saturninus and Bassianus, speaks from above.*

We must now return to the intervening episode, introduced in the Quarto by the direction

Sound Drums and Trumpets, and then enter two of Titus *sonnes, and then two men bearing a Coffin couered with black, then two other sonnes, then* Titus Andronicus, *and then* Tamora *the Queene of Gothes and her two sonnes* Chiron *and* Demetrius, *with* Aron *the More, and others as many as can be, then set downe the Coffin, and* Titus *speakes.*

The main problem with this direction is that it omits Alarbus, who plays a prominent, though non-speaking, part in the ensuing action.

---

[14] The awkwardness would have been less apparent in what appears to have been Shakespeare's original plotting of the scene, omitting the sacrifice of Alarbus: see p. 89.

To be precise, he is donated by Titus to his sons so that they may 'hew his limbs and on a pile, | *Ad manus fratrum*, sacrifice his flesh'. His mother, Tamora, pleads for him in vain, and Lucius orders

> Away with him, and make a fire straight,
> And with our swords vpon a pile of wood,
> Lets hew his limbs till they be cleane consumde,

following which both Quarto and Folio direct the sons to leave '*with Alarbus*'. His omission from the Quarto's entry direction is generally agreed to be the result of a change of plan on Shakespeare's part. According to Marcus, Titus has already 'slaine the Noblest prisoner of the *Gothes*'. Presumably Shakespeare drafted the scene without intending to represent this episode, changed his mind, wrote it in, but did not adjust the direction. The recognition that Alarbus must enter before he can leave was made, creditably but unsurprisingly, by the first of Shakespeare's named editors, Nicholas Rowe. Astonishingly, John Munro argued in the *Times Literary Supplement* of 10 June 1949 that (to quote Maxwell) Alarbus 'was never on the stage at all, and that the mention of him [in the exit direction] . . . is an erroneous addition by "somebody" unspecified'. Still more surprisingly, J. C. Maxwell in his first edition did not add Alarbus' name to the entry direction, even though he made it clear in his note that he did not agree with Munro's argument. Maxwell was one of the best scholars of his generation, but he was also, at least at the time he edited *Titus*, among the more conservative. We have seen that he preferred not to tamper with the Quarto directions, but it is difficult to see how, when he could add '*at the other* [*doore*]' to the opening direction—a phrase which any reader could supply without expert assistance—and could add '*Exeunt the followers of Bassianus*' without apparently having thought very much about who should and who should not be on the stage, and could also add a modified version of Dyce's direction for the entry of Marcus, etc., apparently without seeing that his modification makes nonsense of it—it is difficult to see how this editor could have justified not adding to an entry direction the name of a character who he agrees must enter, and for whom the Quarto itself supplies an exit. And in the same direction, it seems similarly perverse not to add the names of Titus' sons—Martius, Mutius, Lucius, and Quintus—especially as the only one to speak in this episode, Lucius, is not named in the dialogue and is identified in the speech prefixes of the edition only by the abbreviation '*Luc.*', whereas the Quarto at least gives the name in full.

And in this matter, too, Maxwell is inconsistent, because at l. 340, where the Quarto direction reads '*Enter Marcus and Titus sonnes*', Maxwell *does* give their names, in a direction deriving from Capell—*Enter* MARCUS, LUCIUS, QUINTUS, *and* MARTIUS' (Mutius by this time having been killed by his father) while (in his first edition) mistakenly collating '*Enter*' as '*Re-enter*'—probably the relic of a changed intention, but one cannot help feeling that Maxwell was not at his best in editing this scene. Other problems about the mass entry which introduces Titus to the stage concern the number of coffins which should accompany him, and his means of entry. I reserve discussion of the former to the point in the text at which the bodies are interred. As for Titus' means of entry, at a later point in the scene, in gratitude to Saturninus for his proposal to marry Titus' daughter, Lavinia, Titus declares to the Emperor:

> . . . here in sight of Rome to *Saturnine*,
> King and Commander of our common weale,
> The wide worlds Emperour, doe I consecrate
> My sword, my Chariot, and my Prisoners,
> Presents well worthy Romes imperious Lord:
> Receiue them then, the tribute that I owe,
> Mine honours Ensignes humbled at thy feete.

We may expect Titus to have been wearing a sword; I do not feel that it is the editor's duty to specify articles of clothing or equipment which are not out of the ordinary. We know who the prisoners are. But where did the 'chariot' come from? Only one answer, surely, is possible: Titus entered in it, just as Tamburlaine enters in his chariot in *Tamburlaine* Part Two, Act Four, Scene Four. The fact that this is not specified in the direction is irrelevant. There is as much reason to add '*in his chariot*' to this direction as there is to add '*with a basket*' to the direction for the Clown's entry in *Antony and Cleopatra*. An eighteenth-century editor made *that* addition, and all modern editors follow. An eighteenth-century editor did *not* make the addition in *Titus*; neither does any modern editor. I cannot help feeling that if Rowe, Theobald, or Capell had done so, it would have become part of the established text. But it is not too late. (Incidentally, a very similar question arises in Act Five, Scene Two, where the entry direction in both Quarto and Folio reads simply '*Enter Tamora and her two sonnes disguised*', but where Titus later says:

Lo by thy side where Rape and Murder stands,
Now giue some surance that thou art reuenge,
Stab them, or teare them on thy Chariot wheeles.

Here, however, because the presence of the chariot on stage is not essential, and also because Titus is mad, one cannot be so sure that Tamora should enter on wheels.)

Maxwell is unhelpfully faithful to Q again at 1. 141, with the direction '*Enter the sons of Andronicus again*'. Here Riverside names the sons, and also adds '*with their swords bloody*', another helpful direction deriving from Capell. The next direction occurs a few lines later, as Titus' dead sons are laid to rest. '*Sound Trumpets, and lay the Coffin in the Tombe*' reads Q; F varies this, reading '*Flourish. Then Sound Trumpets, and lay the Coffins in the Tombe.*' I take it that '*Flourish*' is most plausibly interpreted as a prompt-book annotation, the addition of a more technical term which nevertheless simply duplicates the Quarto's '*Sound Trumpets*', and that an editor may reasonably prefer Q's formula as being more genuinely Shakespearian. The more interesting variant is Q's '*Coffin*' as opposed to F's '*Coffins*'. Maxwell, in a note on the direction at 1. 69, remarks that 'The singular is surprising . . . since ll. 84, 89, 94 call for a number of corpses. But this is probably how the author envisaged the staging and we cannot safely emend.' This is a minor example of the kind of problem that can arise in a text that has not been polished. The author does seem to have 'envisaged' a 'staging' with only one coffin *as he wrote the direction*; but shortly afterwards he was envisaging more than one corpse. Is this reconcilable with the direction? Were there, for example, coffins large enough to hold more than one of Titus' sons?[15] Not so far as I can discover, and anyhow, to expect '*two Men*' to bear one would seem unreasonable. Recourse to *OED* shows that '*coffin*' was sometimes loosely used for 'bier', but the same objections apply. As McKerrow wrote in his draft note, 'There was certainly more than one son to be buried; on the other hand, if the coffin contained more than one body it would surely have taken more than two men to carry it.' It seems

---

[15] 'Titus brings a coffin from the field with him containing at least two of his sons killed in the wars . . .': G. Harold Metz, 'The Early Staging of *Titus Andronicus*', p. 103. Metz's later remark that 'the Folio's "coffins"' lead to the 'virtually inescapable conclusion that the difference reflects a Jacobean change in the staging' (p. 107) both depends on the hypothesis that the Folio reflects a late staging and implies that the Quarto records an achieved staging rather than a projected one.

strange that Shakespeare should have repeated the singular form in the direction at l. 149, since both the line before the direction and the line after it refer to the fact that this is a multiple burial. It might be a misprint; indeed, were it not for the repeated use of the singular in the earlier direction, one would feel fairly sure that it was.

The problem is, of course, practical, not merely academic. Last time I saw the play the director used a coffin big enough for only one fully-grown son, and my companion remarked on the oddity. In defence of the director I whispered that it reflected a textual discrepancy, but of course this is not an adequate defence. There is no conceivable reason why Shakespeare should have wished to talk of the interment of two (or more sons) yet to provide the means for the burial of only one. A director who is consciously faithful to the apparent discrepancy in the text is taking pedantry to the point of irresponsibility to both author and audience. Trevor Nunn, I find from the prompt-book of his 1972 Royal Shakespeare Company production, used two coffins; Peter Brook, in 1955, had brought on three. If an editor keeps the Quarto's singular form—as most editors do—it is surely his duty to remark on the discrepancy; Riverside does not do so. If his sense of logic gets the better of him, he will be tempted by F's plural form; this could be a compositor's change; the context so urgently demands the plural that anyone of normal intelligence might be expected to adopt it. There is also the possibility, supported by the addition of '*Flourish*', that F's plural derives from the prompt-book. I suppose that modern editors are inhibited from making the change by aware-ness that alteration of this direction necessitates altering the earlier direction, and that there a simple change from singular to plural is not enough: the whole phrase '*two men bearing a Coffin*' calls for change. Is there any reason why we should not emend to '*men bearing coffins*'? The change is surely required by the dialogue; it brings the stage action into line with what everyone would agree to be Shakespeare's demonstrable 'final' intentions in the earliest surviving text (even if we invoke the authority of F, that is to say, we are not importing into Q some optional action which might have been added against Shakespeare's wishes). It is no different in principle from removing a ghost character's entrance, or altering the position of entry of a character when (as happens in *Much Ado About Nothing*, for instance) it is clear that Shakespeare changed his mind during the process of composition about who should take part in a particular scene. We make such changes with confidence because our predecessors made them. Should we ourselves be deterred from making similar changes just because our predecessors failed, in a few instances, to see the need for them?

Somewhat later in the scene the editor is faced with the need for a direct decision about whether to add a Folio direction. After Marcus has proclaimed Saturninus emperor—

> . . . we create
> Lord *Saturninus* Romes great Emperour,
> And say *Long liue our Emperour* Saturnine.
>
> (ll. 231–3)

—Folio adds '*A long Flourish till they come downe*.'. It is a double direction. The flourish is not, perhaps, absolutely indispensable, but it seems entirely natural both to emphasize the importance of the proclamation and to cover the action which forms the second part of the direction, i.e. '*they come downe*'. The flourish is warranted by the Folio, presumably by way of the prompt-book, so I should include it. The direction that '*they come downe*'—that is, that Marcus, Saturninus, Bassianus, and other Tribunes descend from the upper to the lower level — is even more important as confirmation of what is easily to be deduced from the dialogue, which makes it all the more surprising that Maxwell simply collates F's direction without even discussing it. This means that, so far as his stage directions go, Marcus, Bassianus, and the others remain on the upper level, while Lavinia is on the lower level; yet later, after Bassianus lays claim to Lavinia, Maxwell has the direction (reprinted, substantially, from Malone) '*Exeunt Marcus and Bassianus, with Lavinia*'. Riverside adds Folio's direction (as does Bevington). My own inclination would be to signal both the importance of the action and the unauthoritative status of the Folio's wording by rephrasing it in a way which would indicate the required action more clearly, for example '*A· long Flourish while Marcus Andronicus and the other Tribunes, with Saturninus and Bassianus, descend to the lower stage.*' It is also clear that the '*Flourish*' should be accompanied by the acclamations of the spectators to the tune of 'Long live our Emperor Saturnine'; but perhaps this need not be spelt out.

An additional problem, not faced by editors, relates to Marcus' offer to Titus of 'This palliament of white and spotless hue' (Titus rejects the offer). McKerrow, in his unpublished notes, says that this and the reference (l. 184) to 'these our late deceased Emperours sonnes'

make 'clear that these characters at least cannot now have been "aloft"',
but this assumes that the direction for them to 'go up into the Senate
House' (l. 63) implies that they were to pass out of sight, which is not
necessarily so. McKerrow (who has obviously thought harder than most
editors about the staging of the scene) writes as if the Quarto were a
text that records action that took place rather than one written as a
guide for action that would take place. It may well be that Shakespeare
had not fully worked out his staging. But there is no need for Marcus
to be on the same level as Titus in offering him the palliament: an
attendant 'aloft' might bear the imperial insignia (just as Marcus,
earlier, was holding the crown); or it would even be possible for an
attendant to bring them on to the lower stage as Marcus spoke. What
does seem clear is the need for Saturninus to be invested after 'they
come down', so I should add a direction, such as *'Marcus invests
Saturninus in the white palliament and hands him a sceptre'* at this
point (for the sceptre, see l. 199). No editor does so.

A little later in the scene comes an exceptionally interesting episode
which needs to be examined in some detail. Saturninus, having 'come
down', decides, with Titus' approval, to marry Lavinia (who is not
consulted). Titus hands over to him all his prisoners. Titus speaks:

> Now Madam are you prisoner to an Emperour . . .

A small point, but as the last woman to be named was Lavinia, it is
helpful to indicate that this is addressed to Tamora; Riverside does,
Maxwell does not. Next, Saturninus comments on Tamora:

> A goodly Lady trust me of the hue,
> That I would choose were I to choose a new.

These lines are traditionally marked *'aside'*, following Capell; Riverside
follows, Maxwell does not. Here there is something to be said for
Maxwell's break with tradition. The lines might be spoken aside to the
audience; they might be (as they effectively were in John Barton's
production) addressed to Titus, a complaisant evaluation by Saturninus
of his prize; though Saturninus might well not wish Lavinia to hear
them, there is no reason why Tamora should not; and even Lavinia
may be supposed to hear them, since at the end of his speech Saturninus,
after having virtually proposed to Tamora,

> Madam he comforts you,
> Can make you greater than the Queene of *Gothes*,

turns to Lavinia with '*Lauinia* you are not displeasde with this.' Lavinia replies

> Not I my Lord, sith true Nobilitie,
> Warrants these words in Princely curtesie.

Presumably Saturninus supposes that Lavinia has heard his words to Tamora, and may be disturbed by them, and so seeks from Lavinia an assurance, which she provides, that she interprets them more innocently than they are intended. Saturninus is playing a double game, but I think the '*aside*' direction is simplistic, and better omitted.

Next, Saturninus says

> Thanks sweete *Lauinia*, Romans let vs goe,
> Raunsomles here we set our prisoners free,
> Proclaime our Honours Lords with Trumpe and Drum.

Neither Quarto nor Folio follows this with a direction. Following Rowe's wording and Capell's placing, almost all editors add

Flourish. Saturninus courts Tamora in dumb show.

This is presumably to cover the fact that Saturninus says nothing during the following few lines in which Bassianus claims, and seizes, Lavinia, but it is less than satisfactory for two reasons: one, that, having said 'Romans let vs goe', Saturninus does not go; two, that the action the direction demands is imposed on the text. Let us look a little further before returning to this.

The dialogue that follows Saturninus' 'Proclaime our Honours Lords with Trumpe and Drum' is given below exactly as it appears in the Quarto:

> The moſt Lamentable *Tragedie*
> *Lauinia* you are not diſpleaſde with this.
> *Lauinia,* Not I my Lord,ſith true Nobilitie,
> VVarrants theſe words in Princely curteſie.
>   *Saturnine.* Thanks ſweete *Lauinia,*Romans let vs goe,
> Raunſomles here we ſet our priſoners free,
> Proclaime our Honours Lords with Trumpe and Drum.

Baſſianus. Lord *Titus* by your leaue, this maid is mine.
Titus. How ſir, are you in earneſt then my Lord?
Baſcianus. I Noble *Titus* and reſolude withall,
To doo my ſelfe this reaſon and this right.
Marcus. *Suum cuiqum* is our Romane iuſtee,
This Prince in iuſtice ceazeth but his owne.
Lucius. And that he will, and ſhall if *Lucius* liue.
Titus. Traitors auaunt, where is the Emperours gard?
Treaſon my Lord, *Lauinia* is ſurprizde.
Saturnine. Surprizde, by whom?
Baſcianus. By him that iuſtly may,
Beare his betrothde from all the world away.
Mutius. Brothers, helpe to conuay her hence away,
And with my ſword Ile keepe this doore ſafe.
Titus. Follow my Lord, and Ile ſoone bring her backe.
Mutius. My Lord you paſſe not here.
Titus. What villaine boy, barſt me my way in Rome?
Mutius. Helpe *Lucius*, helpe.
Lucius. My Lord you are vniuſt, and more than ſo,
In wrongfull quarrell you haue ſlaine your ſonne.
Titus. Nor thou, nor he, are any ſonnes of mine,
My ſonnes would neuer ſo diſhonour me,
Traitor reſtore *Lauinia* to the Emperour.
Lucius. Dead if you will, but not to be his wife,
That is anothers lawfull promiſt loue.
Enter aloft the Emperour with Tamora and her two
ſonnes and Aron the moore.
Emperour. No *Titus*, no, the Emperour needes her not,
Nor her, nor thee, nor any of thy ſtocke:

Ile

(B3^v; 1.1.270–300)

The stage direction shows that at some point during this dialogue Saturninus and his party must leave the lower stage. It is important to remember that all interpretations of the action required by this dialogue derive from the eighteenth-century editors, except that the Folio adds '*He kils him*' after Mutius' 'Helpe *Lucius*, helpe'—a piece of action which is easily deducible from the words spoken. Before this, the tradition is as follows: Bassianus is '*seizing Lavinia*' (so Riverside, but not Maxwell) as he says 'Lord *Titus* by your leaue, this maid is mine.' This is Rowe's direction; it seems dispensable. Although editors do not instruct Saturninus to *stop* courting Tamora, they imply that he does so on Titus' cry

> Traitors auaunt, where is the Emperours gard?
> Treason my Lord, *Lauinia* is surprizde.

They instruct Bassianus to leave with Marcus (who has supported him) and Lavinia after his declaration that he has a right to 'Beare his betrothde from all the world away.' This too is basically Rowe's direction (Malone added Marcus), followed by both Riverside and Maxwell. It might, I think, equally well be placed after the next two lines, Mutius'

> Brothers, helpe to conuay her hence away,
> And with my sword Ile keepe this doore safe.

At this point editors usually provide a direction for Lucius, Quintus, and Martius to leave. This seems logical enough, though I am not entirely confident that Lucius, at least, should go, since a few moments later Mutius is calling to him for help, so editors who take him off— including Riverside and Arden—have to bring him back again very rapidly.

Titus' next line is crucial: 'Follow my Lord, and Ile soone bring her backe.' Is 'my Lord' an apostrophe to Saturninus? This seems the most natural explanation. It might be the object of 'follow'—'follow my Lord'—but if so, to whom is it addressed? (The theatrical problems of the line are clear from the fact that Peter Brook, in 1955, altered it to 'Fear not, my lord . . . ' and Trevor Nunn, in 1972, to 'Stay here, my lord . . . '!)

After this, obviously, Titus tries to leave in quest of Lavinia and is opposed by Mutius with 'My Lord you passe not here'; Mutius calls to Lucius for help, and, as the Folio (though not the Quarto) says, '*He* [i.e. Titus] *kils him.*'

In the Folio, this episode appears thus:

Mut. **My Lord you paſſe not heere.**
Tit. What villaine Boy, bar'ſt me my way in Rome?
Mut. Helpe *Lucius* helpe.   *He kils him.*
Luc. My Lord you are vniuſt, and more then ſo,
In wrongfull quarrell, you haue ſlaine your ſon.
Tit. Nor thou, nor he are any ſonnes of mine,
My ſonnes would neuer ſo diſhonour me.
Traytor reſtore *Lauinia* to the Emperour.
Luc. Dead if you will, but not to be his wife,
That is anothers lawfull promiſt Loue.

Enter aloft the Emperour with Tamora and her two
ſonnes, and Aaron the Moore.

(cc5; 1.1.290–8)

Clearly the direction '*He kils him*' belongs with Titus' line, yet equally clearly the killing is not completed till Mutius has cried for help. Maxwell observes the Folio's intention, with the unfortunate result— especially since he follows its direction with a long interpolated direction derived substantially from the (old) Cambridge edition—'*During the fray, exeunt Saturninus, Tamora, Demetrius, Chiron and Aaron*' —of making it appear that Mutius' cry is posthumous. Riverside more sensibly prints the direction after the cry and amends to '*Titus kills him.*'

Now we must retrace our steps. I referred earlier to Saturninus' lines

> Thanks sweete *Lauinia*, Romans let vs goe,
> Raunsomles here we set our prisoners free,
> Proclaime our Honours Lords with Trumpe and Drum.
>   (ll. 273–5)

I remarked that neither Quarto nor Folio follows this with a direction, but that editors conventionally add '*Flourish. Saturninus courts Tamora in dumb show*'; and I commented that this is not entirely satisfactory. I find that one respected editor did in fact question this interpretation of the staging, but that, though his view of it has reached print, it was not published. It is clear from R. B. McKerrow's unpublished text of the play (referred to in my Preface) that he rethought this episode. Instead of adopting the direction for Saturninus to 'court Tamora in dumb show', at this point McKerrow adds an exit direction for the imperial party: '*Exeunt Saturninus, Tamora, her two sons, and Aron.*' It is logical enough except that Saturninus has to speak ten lines later: 'Treason my Lord', says Titus, '*Lauinia* is surprizde.' 'Surprizde, by whom?' says Saturninus. McKerrow gets over the difficulty by marking Saturninus' speech '*within*'. In his note, McKerrow justifies his decision thus: 'As a general rule . . . when a character says "let us go", he goes and it seems to me probable that Saturninus and his group really leave the stage after l. 278 [275]. At l. 287 [i.e. 'Treason my Lord . . .'] Titus calls to the Emperor who is, I think, within or appears momentarily above. Probably the former is intended as it is hardly reasonable to suppose that if he were in a position to see what is passing he would not have said something beyond a vague "Surprizde, by whom".' This is ingenious; an objection that McKerrow seems not to have considered is that Titus' 'Follow my Lord, and Ile soone bring her backe', spoken three and a half lines after Saturninus' 'Surprizde, by whom?' is also most naturally interpreted as addressed to Saturninus, who would have to appear more than 'momentarily' above to justify it. Conceivably McKerrow thought of it as addressed to Lucius, whom he does not take off with Quintus and Martius; but it would seem odd for Titus to address his son as 'my lord'.

We can now return to the last few lines of this passage. The conventional way (deriving from the old Cambridge edition) of preparing for the re-entry of the imperial party 'aloft' is to instruct them to leave the main stage during the fight in which Titus kills Mutius: '*During the fray, exeunt Saturninus, Tamora, Demetrius, Chiron, and Aaron*' (so Arden and Riverside). If accurate, it is poor stagecraft. This is, alas, not impossible. The uncertainties of this passage are of the kind that it is easy to associate with a foul-papers text, and they may result partly from revision in the course of composition: it is generally agreed that the sacrifice of Alarbus, earlier in the scene, is an addition; Dover Wilson plausibly argued that the later episode of the burial of Mutius is another; and if this is so, then it is not improbable that, as Wilson also suspected (p. xxxvi), the slaying of Mutius, too, is an addition; he is, as Wilson says, 'a quite unnecessary complication'; moreover, and in spite of the fate in store for Aaron, people are usually dead before they are buried, and if Shakespeare, in his earlier draft, had killed Mutius he would probably also have arranged to dispose of him. Some support for this suggestion might be found in the smoothness of the transition from Titus' 'Follow my Lord, and Ile soone bring her backe' to the first line of Saturninus' speech after the direction for him to enter 'aloft': 'No *Titus*, no, the Emperour needes her not.' We can, therefore, posit an original version reading as follows:

Saturnine. Thanks sweete *Lauinia*, Romans let vs goe,
 Raunsomles here we set our prisoners free,
 Proclaime our Honours Lords with Trumpe and Drum.
     [*Exeunt* intended, but not marked in the manuscript.]
Bassianus. Lord *Titus* by your leaue, this maid is mine.
Titus. How sir, are you in earnest then my Lord?
Bascianus. I Noble *Titus* and resolude withall,
 To doo my selfe this reason and this right.
Marcus. Suum cuique is our Romane iustice,
 This Prince in iustice ceazeth but his owne.
Lucius. And that he will, and shall if *Lucius* liue.
Titus. Traitors auaunt, where is the Emperours gard?
   [*Enter aloft the Emperour with Tamora and her two sonnes*
   and Aron the moore.]
 Treason my Lord, *Lauinia* is surprizde.
Saturnine. Surprizde, by whom?
Bascianus. By him that iustly may,
 Beare his betrothde from all the world away.
   [*Exeunt* for Bassianus, Marcus, Lavinia, and Titus' sons intended
   but not written in the manuscript.]
Titus [*to Saturninus*]. Follow my Lord, and Ile soone bring her backe.
Emperour. No *Titus*, no, the Emperour needes her not,
 Nor her, nor thee, nor any of thy stocke . . .

This version has Saturninus leave at his obvious exit cue and reappear at the point when he is subsequently addressed, as well as providing an obvious cue for his next speech ('No *Titus* . . .'). The revision, as printed in the Quarto, has the difficulty that Saturninus has to speak his apparent exit cue, then to speak the words that McKerrow conjectured to be '*within*', and then to reappear '*above*'. This problem can be overcome by supposing that, on deciding to add the killing of Mutius, Shakespeare intended to delay Saturninus' re-entry so as to avoid his being a mute spectator of this event, and so marked for omission the brief exchange involving the Emperor, but that these lines were mistakenly included in the Quarto. The revised version as intended would then have run as above for the first six speeches (up to Lucius' 'And that he will, and shall if *Lucius* liue.'), and then:

Titus. Traitors auaunt, where is the Emperours gard?
Mutius. Brothers, helpe to conuay her hence away,
　And with my sword Ile keepe this doore safe.
　　[*Exeunt* for Bassianus, Marcus, Lavinia, and Titus' sons (perhaps
　　excluding Lucius) intended but not written in the manuscript.]
Titus. Follow my Lord, and Ile soone bring her backe.
Mutius. My Lord . . .

The absence of Saturninus deprives Titus' 'Follow my Lord' of its obvious addressee in the earlier version, but it could easily enough have been spoken to a bystanding nobleman. Indeed, the line would come even better at the end of the episode, as a cue for Saturninus' 'No *Titus*, no, the Emperour needes her not', and it is tempting to speculate that the confusion in the manuscript caused by the adding of Mutius' killing caused it to be misplaced.

So complex a set of issues requires some sort of summing-up. If the version of the scene as printed in 1594 is held to be substantially correct, with Saturninus remaining on stage after his apparent exit cue, I think, as I have said, that the editor should drop the Rowe–Capell direction for him to speak 'aside' to Tamora following this. I do not find McKerrow's exit direction at l. 275 compatible with Q's dialogue as it stands, since it seems implausible that Saturninus should speak 'Surprizde, by whom?' off stage and because Titus' 'Follow my Lord . . .' seems most naturally addressed to Saturninus. So I should have to accede in the traditional direction for the imperial party to depart during or after Titus' killing of Mutius. I should move the direction for the flight of Bassianus, Marcus, and Lavinia from its traditional placing at l. 286 to two lines later, where they must be joined also by Quintus and Martius, but I should leave Lucius on stage, along with Mutius, so that he is not required to make a rapid re-entry, and also since it seems more plausible for Mutius to call on this particular brother if he is on stage than if he is not. If, however, the revision theory posited here is accepted (and I should stress that it implies revision during, not after, composition), then I should re-arrange the text along the lines suggested. The edited episode would then read (in modern spelling):

Saturninus. Thanks, sweet Lavinia. Romans, let us go.
　Ransomless here we set our prisoners free.
　Proclaim our honours, lords, with trump and drum!

Exeunt Saturninus, Tamora, Demetrius, Chiron, and Aaron

Bassianus. Lord Titus, by your leave, this maid is mine.

Titus. How, sir, are you in earnest, then, my lord?

Bassianus. Ay, noble Titus, and resolved withal
   To do myself this reason and this right.

Marcus. Suum cuique is our Roman justice.
   This prince in justice seizeth but his own.

Lucius. And that he will, and shall, if Lucius live.

Titus. Traitors, avaunt! Where is the Emperor's guard?

Mutius. Brothers, help to convey her hence away,
   And with my sword I'll keep this door safe.

   Exeunt Bassianus, Marcus, Lavinia, Quintus, and Martius
   (*To Titus*) My lord, you pass not here.

Titus. What, villain boy, barr'st me my way in Rome?
   He attacks Mutius

Mutius. Help, Lucius, help!   *He dies*

Lucius (*to Titus*). My lord, you are unjust, and more than so,
   In wrongful quarrel you have slain your son.

Titus. Nor thou nor he are any sons of mine.
   My sons would never so dishonour me.
   Traitor, restore Lavinia to the Emperor.

Lucius. Dead, if you will, but not to be his wife
   That is another's lawful promised love.   *exit*

   *Enter aloft Saturninus with Tamora, Chiron, Demetrius, and
   Aaron the Moor*

Titus. Follow, my lord, and I'll soon bring her back.

Saturninus. No, Titus, no. The Emperor needs her not . . .

The scene proceeds, with Saturninus and his party on the upper level
addressing Titus on the main stage.

In this episode, too, piecemeal composition might be suspected.
Towards the end of the passage I have just quoted, Lucius accuses
Titus of injustice in killing Mutius, and Titus disowns sons who would
'dishonour' him. Then follows the self-contained, upper-level episode,
after which the substance of this interchange is repeated, this time
between Marcus and Titus. Like Lucius, Marcus points out to Titus
that he has killed his son:

> O *Titus* see: O see what thou has done
> In a bad quarrell slaine a vertuous sonne.

Titus again disowns those who, he believes, have dishonoured him:

No foolish Tribune, no: No sonne of mine,
Nor thou, nor these, confederates in the deede,
That hath dishonoured all our Familie,
Vnworthy brother, and vnworthy sonnes.

And we move into the episode in which Marcus and his nephews persuade Titus to allow Mutius' burial. It is an oddity of the stagecraft that, so far as the directions in the Quarto and all later editions are concerned, Mutius' body has had to remain, ignored, on stage throughout the upper-level episode.[16] That episode merely makes explicit what is already implicit—that Saturninus is taking Tamora to himself—and it would be easy to believe that Shakespeare originally intended to move straight from the killing of Mutius to his burial; but this conflicts with the notion, also plausible, that the killing and burial of Mutius are themselves interpolations. Shakespeare could not have interpolated a scene into one that was not written, and I cannot see how the action could have passed from Bassianus' seizing of Lavinia to the episode which now follows Mutius' burial, because by then Bassianus is claiming to have married Lavinia. The problem is resolved, however, if we make the quite reasonable assumption that Mutius' body should not remain on stage, but should be dragged off by Lucius after the killing (l. 298) and carried back again by Marcus, or by one or more of the sons, on the line 'O *Titus* see: O see what thou hast done' (l. 341), a line which would gain immeasurably in effectiveness if Marcus were not pointing to a body which had been lying around the stage throughout the previous episode but perhaps carrying his nephew's corpse as Lear, later, was to carry the dead Cordelia. It is true that Shakespeare appears not to have written directions for these happenings, but neither did he write directions for Martius and Quintus to fall into the pit (2.3.197, 245), for Chiron and Demetrius to carry off the Nurse's body (4.2.172), for the bringing on of a ladder and Aaron's ascent of it (5.1.53), for Titus to kill Lavinia (5.3.46), for Saturninus to kill Titus (5.3.64), and for Lucius to kill Saturninus (5.3.66)—to give only a few examples of deficiencies at points where the action is undisputed. If this interpretation of the action is granted, the repetitions of the rebukes to Titus and his self-defence may seem simply a way of recalling the situation to the audience's mind.

Another anomaly which has been explained as a result of the rewriting follows Mutius' burial. After his uncle and brothers have paid

---

[16] Peter Brook, in his famous production (Stratford-upon-Avon, 1955), had Mutius buried as soon as killed and omitted most of the pleading on his behalf.

their tribute comes the direction *'Exit all but Marcus and Titus'* (l. 37). Yet later in the scene the Quarto ascribes to Tamora a speech in which the last three lines come inappropriately from her; in the Folio they are ascribed to *'Son'*. The Quarto reads:

> And feare not Lords, and you *Lauinia,*
> By my aduife all humbled on your knees,
> You fhall aske pardon of his Maieftie.
> VVee doo, and vowe to Heauen and to his Highnes,
> That what wee did, was mi'd ie as we might,
> Tendring our fifters honour and our owne.

(C2ᵛ; 1.1.471-6)

There is no reason to doubt the Folio prefix, which was adopted by Rowe (working, of course, from a Folio reprint) and interpreted as 'Lucius'. But the anomaly in the Quarto has been explained by the hypothesis that when the burial of Mutius was added the episodes were not brought fully into consonance with one another. In order to leave the necessary sons on the stage, Rowe deleted the direction *'Exit all but Marcus and Titus'*, and is followed by most editors, including Maxwell, but not by Riverside, which follows Kittredge in printing '[*They rise, and*] *all but Marcus and Titus* [*stand aside*].' McKerrow had had similar thoughts, conjecturing that the Quarto direction 'may represent the writer's first intention modified in the course of composition, or some larger readjustment, perhaps bound up with the omission of the speech before ["We doo, and vowe to Heauen ..."]'. It is possible that, as Shakespeare wrote the interpolated episode of Mutius' burial, he forgot that he needed to leave Titus' sons on stage; if so, Kittredge's modification of Rowe seems acceptable, even though it leaves the director with the difficult task of deciding what to do with the spare sons. McKerrow conjectures that they may 'have retired to the back of the stage to close the tomb'. Another possibility is that they are 'the others' mentioned in the entry direction at the start of the following episode—'*Enter . . . Bascianus and Lauinia, with others*'; though this seems an oddly vague way of referring to them, for, as they were associated with Bassianus and Lavinia at their last appearance, when Titus killed Mutius, they are the most obvious characters to reappear with them.

A minor problem, but one which recurs, with variations, in many plays, occurs towards the end of the burial episode. Titus has been reluctantly persuaded to allow Mutius' body to 'be buried with his brethren'. 'Well burie him, and burie me the next' says Titus, ungraciously (l. 386). A direction in the Quarto reads *'they put him in the tombe'*; it is not clear, and is not very important, exactly who is signified here by *'they'*, but it seems unlikely that Titus has an active hand in the burial. Then Lucius says

> There lie thy bones sweete *Mutius* with thy friends,
> Till wee with Trophees doo adorne thy tombe.

This is followed by the direction

> *they all kneele and say*,
> No man shed teares for Noble *Mutius*,
> He liues in fame, that dide in vertues cause.

There is no speech prefix for this epitaph; editors usually replace the direction by the prefix 'ALL' followed by '(*kneeling*)'—so Maxwell; Riverside prints Quarto's direction as a prefix. But I find it very difficult to believe that the truculent Titus is intended to join in the chorus, any more than that he should help to bury Mutius, so I should be inclined to read, not *'All'*, but *'All but Titus'*, or words to that effect.[17]

More unsignalled action occurs in the last stretch of the scene. Tamora intercedes with Saturninus to appear to forgive Titus and restore him to favour. 'Rise Titus rise, my Empresse hath preuaild', says Saturninus (l. 459), though we have had no instruction for Titus to kneel. Most editors, including Riverside and Arden, also give no instructions. There is, admittedly, no point at which it is evident that Titus kneels; but he cannot rise unless he has knelt, and I favour Bevington's decision to select the most plausible point (at the end of l. 427), and add instructions for him to kneel there and to rise on Saturninus' command. Titus' kneeling, clearly demanded by the text, gains ironic significance when seen as a reversal of the situation at l. 104, when Tamora, pleading for her sons, surely must kneel too, as she does in the Peacham drawing, though editors also fail to mark

---

[17] E. A. J. Honigmann discusses *'All'* speeches in his article referred to on p. 77, but is not concerned there with the problem of whether 'All' should exclude certain characters who are nevertheless on stage. He usefully points to the need to consider whether 'speeches ascribed to *"All"*', or to an indefinite number of speakers' should be spoken in chorus, whether they should be allocated to different consecutive speakers, or even whether they should be taken to indicate 'simultaneous "confused" speech'.

this. Similarly a few lines later: addressing Bassianus, Marcus, Titus'
sons, and Lavinia, Tamora says

> . . . feare not Lords, and you *Lauinia*,
> By my advise all humbled on your knees,
> You shall aske pardon of his Maiestie.

'Wee doo', says a 'Son' (in the Folio); a little later Tamora says to
Saturninus 'The Tribune and his Nephews kneele for grace . . .', and
Saturninus responds to her appeal with

> Marcus, for thy sake, and thy brothers here,
> And at my louelie *Tamoras* intreats,
> I doo remit these young mens hainous faults,
> Stand vp . . .

Arden has no directions. Riverside sensibly adds the appropriate ones,
attributing the former to one 'Witherspoon (*after Collier*)', and the
second to 'Chambers (*subs.*)'.

We do not encounter the final problem in this problematical scene
until we reach its last line; then, in fact, part of the problem is whether
this really is its last line. Titus invites Saturninus to hunt with him.
Saturninus accepts, and the Quarto calls for all but Aaron to leave
the stage:

(C2ᵛ; 1.1.492–2.1.2)

There is, that is, no pause in the action, and no apparent change in
location: in other words, no scene break.

The Folio, however, calls for a general exit, marks an act break,
and instructs Aaron to re-enter:

Tit. To morrow and it pleafe your Maieftie,
To hunt the Panther and the Hart with me,
With horne and Hound,
Weele giue your Grace *Bon iour,*
Satur. Be it fo *Titus,*and Gramercy to.. *Exeunt.*

Actus Secunda.

Flourifh. *Enter Aaron alone.*

Aron. Now climbeth *Tamora* Olympus toppe,

(cc6; 1.1.492–2.1.1)

The two printings imply different stagings of the scene; the crucial question is whether the Folio's alterations have theatrical warrant, or whether they are adjustments consequent upon an imposition of act breaks made in the printing-house only. The Riverside editor, placing his faith in the Quarto, notes *'there is no act or scene break here, Aaron remaining on stage'*, while adding a centred heading '[ACT II, SCENE 1]'. A more logical procedure would have been to abandon the act and scene break altogether. This, of course, entails the inconvenience of sabotaging the conventional system of reference; the least unsatisfactory compromise is achieved by those editors who treat act and scene divisions as mere conveniences, to be printed unobtrusively in the margin, rather in Dover Wilson's manner.

Other editors, however, pay more attention to the Folio; thus, Maxwell prints a mixture of the two, giving *'Sound trumpets. Exeunt all but Aaron'* at the end of Act One, which (following the conventions of the series) is made to end a page. On the following page he prints a prominent act/scene heading, followed by simply *'Aaron alone'*. His note at the end of Act One reads 'The Q S.D. shows that II.i is continuous in action with Act I. F's "Flourish", after "Actus Secunda" [*sic*] is clearly misplaced from the end of Act I.' Maxwell is surely right in following Capell's replacing of the direction for trumpets to call *before* the *Exeunt*; Riverside offers no explanation of its break from sound editorial tradition here. Clearly, too, Maxwell recognized that so far as the Quarto is concerned, an act break is out of place, even though the conventions of the series to which he was contributing required him to give undue prominence to it.[18]

Nevertheless, there are grounds for supposing that the Folio represents, not merely a printing-house imposition upon the text, but a change in staging introduced after the play had been produced. '*Flourish*' instead of '*Sound trumpets*' replaces a literary by a theatrical term, and so suggests prompt-book influence; the replacement of '*manet* Moore' by '*Enter Aaron alone*' also may suggest recourse to a manuscript rather than readjustment based on the Quarto alone. Shakespeare may have had second thoughts about Aaron's remaining on stage: the suggestion of a break in time adds to the plausibility of the action, and would have been convenient if a structure representing a tomb had had to be removed. The so-called law of re-entry seems to have been relaxed when act breaks were observed, as they commonly were in Shakespeare's theatre from about 1607 (as between Acts Four and Five of *The Tempest*), so this alteration, at least, appears to be a late one. An editor who follows the Quarto here, then, is not necessarily misrepresenting the play as acted, but to follow the Folio is more consistent with the general policy of accepting the Folio's act divisions.

In discussing the first act of *Titus Andronicus*, I have dealt empirically with a variety of features to which the editor needs to devote his attention. Some of my comments affect no more than mechanical aspects of presentation. But others, I think, help to show that this long span of action is a more consciously wrought and sophisticated piece of dramatic artistry than is usually granted, and in particular that it employs visual effects to convey and reinforce meaning. If, following the Folio, we allow Marcus to make an individual entry with the crown at l. 17, rather than have him enter at the start of the play as one of a group, we give greater initial prominence to one of the play's central characters, and lay emphasis upon an emblem of the sovereignty which is disputed in the opening episodes. If we clarify the action at l. 63, where Saturninus and Bassianus '*goe vp into the Senate house*',

[18] Greg, in his review, was unfair in remarking that Maxwell 'allows the Moor to remain on the stage during the interval'. Maxwell makes quite clear in his note that no 'interval' is implied.

we make it more obvious that the scene draws on the popular conventions of the 'siege' scene. If we make clear that Titus should make his
entrance, at l. 69, in a chariot, we align him with the visual presentation
of triumphant conquerors in such earlier plays as Marlowe's *Tamburlaine*
Part Two and in Gascoigne and Kinwelmersh's *Jocasta*,[19] and make
explicit, too, a foreshadowing of the account of Tamora with a
triumphal chariot at the opening of Act Five, Scene Two. If we add a
direction for the investment of Saturninus at l. 233, we show the
formal, ritualistic resolution of the problem of the succession with
which the play opened. If we allow that Lucius should remove Mutius'
body at l. 298, we avoid the awkwardness of supposing that the body
should remain, ignored, on stage throughout the subsequent episode;
then if we follow this, as we must, by having Marcus or his nephews
carry in the body at l. 340, we reveal an addition to the play's moving
tableaux of grief. And if we provide instructions for Tamora to kneel
at l. 104 as she pleads to Titus on her sons' behalf, and for Titus to
kneel while Tamora hypocritically and falsely pleads with Saturninus
on his behalf (ll. 428–58), we give point to the ironic reversal in their
situations. Most of these editorial procedures depend on straightforward
deductions based on information supplied by the text itself; only those
relating to the episode of Lavinia's abduction and the subsequent
killing of Mutius seem to me to be at all speculative in the solutions
they offer to problems which earlier editors have attempted only
half-heartedly to solve. They may not exhibit Shakespeare's intentions
in their final form, but I hope they show that investigation of the
theatrical implications of the texts as originally printed has not been
exhausted, and that it is an integral part of the editor's responsibility.
If we alter and supplement the original directions at all, we should try
to do so systematically and in a manner that draws on all the information provided by the dialogue as well as the directions of the original
editions, and by what we know of the stages for which the plays
were designed.

I have said that the solutions offered to the problems posed by the
episode of Lavinia's abduction are speculative. The episode is patently
unsatisfactory as it stands in both the Quarto and the Folio. In a
modern edition, it might be reprinted exactly as it stands in either of
these texts. This would be the course of the editor of a diplomatic
edition; not even the most conservative of modern editors adopts it.

[19] See, for example, Dieter Mehl, *The Elizabethan Dumb Show* (London,
1965), p. 43.

It might be printed with directions attempting, in the more traditional manner, to make sense of the dialogue as it stands. This is the course adopted by all modern editors, though they vary somewhat in the details of what they add. Or the passage might be printed with a fresh attempt to make sense of it, as McKerrow planned to do, and as is suggested above.

Although a radical change might be resisted, other alterations now accepted have been based on exactly the same principle. In this very scene of *Titus* itself, the three and a half lines of the First Quarto telling of Titus' 'sacrifice of expiation' have frequently been omitted because they conflict with the dramatization of this sacrifice later in the scene. This omission, countenanced on the hypothesis of revision during composition, was first made in the Second Quarto; no doubt this precedent, along with the fact that no copy of the quarto containing the lines was known till 1904, has eased its acceptance by many modern editors; but if it is legitimate, then the proposed change later in the scene is equally so.

No one attempting to make sense of the passage could avoid using, in one form or another, the information provided by the only direction added in the Folio ('*He kils him*', l. 291), information which would inevitably be provided even if the Folio did not exist. There are, however, many other cases, as I have shown, in which the Folio provides information which is not straightforwardly deducible from the quarto, and this is true of all the plays that survive in collateral substantive texts. It returns us to a question which I raised earlier (p. 81): 'Do we prefer the play a little undercooked, perhaps even half-baked, or do we like it in a more finished form, even if a hand other than the author's may have added some of the icing?'

At one time, it was the general assumption that the Folio provided the most authoritative text of all Shakespeare's plays, even those that exist also in quartos printed during his lifetime. During the present century, work inaugurated by A. W. Pollard and others has helped to sort out the good quartos from the bad, and to demonstrate that, for plays printed in quarto, the compilers of the Folio often relied on the earlier printed text as their basic copy. We have learnt, too, that the Folio editors, or their agents, modified the quartos before setting up the Folio text from them. In *Titus Andronicus* Maxwell assumes, but does not argue, that the modifications—which include the addition of an entire scene—derive from a manuscript prompt-book. Reviewing Maxwell's edition, Greg denies the validity of this assumption, suggesting that the additional scene 'need not have formed part of a complete manuscript of the play', and that 'Changes in the directions may be editorial'. Earlier, in *The Editorial Problem*, Greg had written that 'the folio alterations are for the most part due to the editor or compositor, the additions to the book-keeper' (p. 177). Invoking 'the book-keeper' reads like a way of admitting theatrical influence without having it derive from the original prompt-book; Greg had to postulate that 'owing presumably to the loss of the original promptbook, a copy of one of the later quartos had been used and annotated in the theatre, and that this was at the disposal of the printer of F' (p. 120). This is intended to account for what Greg sees as the odd situation that 'a prompt-manuscript ... would necessarily have contained' correct readings corrupted in the Quarto (Q3) from which the Folio text was set up, and that 'in no case was the original reading restored in F'. It pushes Greg to the belief that the 'fly' scene dates from after 1600, when Q2 (in which the corrupt readings first appear) was printed. Essentially, Greg's case that the copy of Q3 used for the Folio was not collated against an authoritative manuscript rests on the fact that the collation has not been as thorough as it undoubtedly would have been if the collator had been W. W. Greg. This is part of a general pattern in Greg's thought; I have argued against it elsewhere in relation to *Love's Labour's Lost*.[20] As Dover Wilson wrote (p. 97 of his edition), the annotator 'was not a modern editor but a seventeenth-century scrivener anxious to finish off a wearisome task'. And since Greg wrote, numerous other studies, pre-eminently J. K. Walton's *The Quarto Copy for the First Folio of Shakespeare* (Dublin, 1971), have demonstrated that there *is* evidence for collation with prompt-books, and that such collation was rarely if ever more than casual and sporadic.

Nevertheless, there remains among editors a predisposition to retreat to the authority of a good quarto even when they agree—as Maxwell did—that the Folio provides information deriving from the theatre. The position is understandable but not unimpugnable. It appears to be based on the desire, as Garrick put it, to 'lose no drop of that immortal man', and to catch his entire output as it was before it entered the theatrical O and, in fertilization, lost its singleness yet fulfilled its destiny. It is a comfortable attitude for editors, because it often precludes the need for difficult decisions. It is, as I have suggested, entirely acceptable in editions whose specific, declared aim

[20] Stanley Wells, 'The Copy for the Folio Text of *Love's Labour's Lost*', *Review of English Studies* NS 33 (1982), 137–47.

is to investigate the quarto text alone. But I do not find it acceptable in editions whose aim is to present the reader with as full and authentic a version as possible of the play that Shakespeare wrote. Nor do I see any consistency in an editorial tradition which allows us to accept and act upon the hypothesis that Shakespeare altered his original conception when his first and second thoughts sit side by side in a single text (as in the duplicated passages at the end of Act Two, Scene Two and the opening of Act Two, Scene Three of *Romeo and Juliet,* or in Act Four, Scene Three and Act Five, Scene Two of *Love's Labour's Lost,* or in the opening speeches of *Titus Andronicus*), but which does not allow us to admit the hypothesis of Shakespearian revision when the first and second thoughts occur in different texts (like the quarto and Folio *King Lear, Troilus and Cressida,* or *Titus Andronicus*). Of all authors Shakespeare least deserves this treatment. He dedicated his life to the theatre. His involvement in it appears, to a degree which may even seem culpable, to have excluded all concern with the publication of his works by any process other than performance. For all, or virtually all, of his career he worked with a single company, in which his position was so strong that it is hard to imagine him being overruled against his better judgement. His colleagues went to a surprising amount of trouble—if not as much as we might have wished— to represent the plays as they were acted. I suggest that whenever we have as authoritative texts a quarto based on foul papers and a Folio text which appears to be reprinted either from a quarto annotated from a theatrical manuscript, or directly from a theatrical manuscript, then the basic editorial procedure to be followed in a fully edited version for the general reader should be to accept the evidence offered by the Folio that supplements or substantially replaces that offered by the quarto.

This procedure may not appeal to everyone. Some readers may, quite legitimately, desire an edited version of the text that lies closest to Shakespeare's manuscript. There is no reason why editors should not provide such texts, so long as they are clear that this is what they are doing. I return, in closing, to words by McKerrow that I quoted in my opening pages: 'there might, I suppose, be at least half a dozen editions of the works of Shakespeare executed on quite different lines, each of which, to one group of readers, would be the best edition possible' (*Prolegomena,* p. 1). This is a wise recognition of the admissibility of diversity. Problems arise when editors allow themselves to be pulled in several directions at once: when they modernize most spelling and punctuation but try 'to preserve a selection of Elizabethan spelling forms that reflect, or may reflect, a distinctive contemporary pronunciation'; when they admit some conjectural emendations but reject others because, while admitting that 'The metre and presumably the text, is defective . . . it is impossible to choose' between other editors' suggested ways of improving it; when they add directions for action that have been proposed by early editors but do not add similar directions at points where those editors failed to see the need for them; and when they are inconsistent in admitting modifications to a basic control text from a collaterally substantive one. If we free ourselves from the illusion (encouraged by W. W. Greg, great scholar though he was) that there is one, and only one, 'right' way to edit Shakespeare, and acknowledge that the texts are open to different kinds of editorial treatment according to the varying needs of those who read them, we shall succeed better in our more limited aims.

APPENDIX

Shakespeare's First Draft of Act One of *Titus Andronicus*: A Conjectural Reconstruction

The following version of Act One of *Titus Andronicus* follows the text of the First Quarto (1594) but omits the passages which there is reason to believe that Shakespeare added after his initial act of composition, that is, the episode of the sacrifice of Alarbus (ll. 96–149 in Alexander's edition), Mutius' attempt to assist Bassianus in abducting Lavinia and Titus' killing of him (ll. 287–8, 289–98), the burial of Mutius (ll. 341–90), and Bassianus' subsequent allusion to the killing (l. 418). All but the last are discussed in Chapter 4 above. The last occurs in lines in which Bassianus defends Titus to Saturnine:

> This Noble Gentleman Lord *Titus* here,
> Is in opinion and in honour wrongd,
> That in the rescue of *Lauinia*,
> With his owne hand did slay his youngest sonne,
> In zeale to you, and highly moude to wrath,
> To be controwld in that he frankelie gaue.
>
> (ll. 415–420)

Possibly Shakespeare had made the alterations before he wrote this entire episode. But Titus' attempt to save Lavinia for Saturnine even in the hypothetical unrevised version would afford grounds enough for Bassianus' defence, and the line 'With his owne hand did slay his youngest sonne' may simply be a replacement for some such words as 'Did bravely venture life and limbs and all.'

Editing has been deliberately conservative: this is, in fact, an attempt at the kind of diplomatic editing alluded to in Chapter 3 above (p. 63). Line numbers are to this version. Emended words are in square brackets, as are additions to stage directions and a line (288) added from the First Folio. The positioning of speech prefixes is regularized and they are expanded in angle brackets but not otherwise normalized. Substantive and incidental emendations are listed at the end.

Enter the Tribunes *and* Senatours *aloft*: *And then enter*
Saturninus *and his followers at one dore, and* Bassianus *and*
his followers, with Drums and Trumpets [, *at another dore*].
Saturninus. Noble *Patricians*, Patrons of my Right,
  Defend the iustice of my cause with armes.
  And Countrimen my louing followers,
  Plead my successiue Title with your swords:
  I am his first borne sonne, that was the last
  That ware the Imperiall Diademe of Rome,
  Then let my Fathers honours liue in me,
  Nor wrong mine age with this indignitie.
Bassianus. Romaines, friends, followers, fauourers of my Right,   10
  If euer *Bassianus Ceasars* sonne,
  Were gratious in the eyes of Royall Rome,
  Keepe then this passage to the Capitoll,
  And suffer not dishonour to approch,
  The Imperiall seate to vertue consecrate,
  To iustice, continence, and Nobillitie:
  But let desert in pure election shine,
  And Romaines fight for freedome in your choice.
     Marcus Andronicus with the Crowne.
[*Marcus.*] Princes that striue by factions and by friends,
  Ambitiously for Rule and Emperie,
  Know that the people of Rome for whom we stand   20
  A speciall Partie, haue by common voice,
  In election for the Romaine Empery
  Chosen *Andronicus*, surnamed *Pius*:
  For many good and great deserts to Rome,
  A Nobler man, a brauer Warriour,
  Liues not this day within the Cittie walls.
  Hee by the Senate is accited home,
  From weary warres against the barbarous *Gothes*,
  That with his sonnes a terrour to our foes,
  Hath yoakt a Nation strong, traind vp in Armes.   30
  Tenne yeares are spent since first he vndertooke
  This cause of Rome, and chastised with armes
  Our enemies pride: Fiue times he hath returnd
  Bleeding to Rome, bearing his valiant sonnes,
  In Coffins from the field, and at this day,
  To the Monument of [y^e] *Andronicy*
  Done sacrifice of expiation,
  And slaine the Noblest prisoner of the *Gothes*.
  And now at last laden with honours spoiles,

Returnes the good *Andronicus* to Rome,   40
Renowned *Titus* flourishing in Armes.
Let vs intreat by honour of his name,
Whom worthily you would haue now succeede,
And in the Capitall and Senates Right,
Whom you pretend to honour and adore,
That you withdraw you, and abate your strength,
Dismisse your followers, and as suters should,
Pleade your deserts in peace and humblenes.
Saturninus. How faire the Tribune speakes to calme my thoughts.
Bassianus. Marcus Andronicus, so I doe affie,   50
In thy vprightnes and integritie,
And so I loue and honour thee and thine,
Thy Noble brother *Titus* and his sonnes,
And her to whom my thoughts are humbled all,
Gratious *Lauinia*, Romes rich ornament,
That I will here dismisse my louing friends:
And to my fortunes and the peoples fauour,
Commit my cause in ballance to be waid.   *Exit Soldiers.*
Saturninus. Friends that haue beene thus forward in my right,
I thanke you all, and here dismisse you all,   60
And to the loue and fauour of my Countrie,
Commit my selfe, my person, and the cause: [*Exeunt Soldiers.*]

Rome be as iust and gratious vnto me,
As I am confident and kinde to thee.
Open the gates and let me in.
Bassianus. Tribunes and me a poore Competitor.
                                    They goe vp into the Senate house.
        Enter a Captaine.
[*Captaine.*] Romaines make way, the good *Andronicus*,
Patron of vertue, Romes best Champion:
Succesfull in the battailes that he fights,
With honour and with fortune is returnd,   70
From where he circumscribed with his sword,
And brought to yoake the enemies of Rome.

        Sound Drums and Trumpets, and then enter two of Titus
        sonnes, and then two men bearing a Coffin couered with black,
        then two other sonnes, then Titus Andronicus, *and then*
        Tamora *the Queene of Gothes and her two sonnes* Chiron *and*
        Demetrius, *with* Aron *the More, and others as many as can be,*
        then set downe the Coffin, and Titus *speakes.*

Titus. Haile Rome, victorious in thy mourning weeds,
    Lo as the Barke that hath discharged his fraught,
    Returnes with pretious lading to the bay,
    From whence at first shee wayd her anchorage;
    Commeth *Andronicus*, bound with Lawrell bowes,
    To resalute his Countrie with his teares,
    Teares of true ioy for his returne to Rome,
    Thou great defender of this Capitoll,   80
    Stand gratious to the rights that we entend.
    Romaines, of fiue and twenty valiant sonnes,
    Halfe of the number that king *Priam* had,
    Behold the poore remaines aliue and dead:
    These that suruiue, let Rome reward with loue:
    These that I bring vnto their latest home,
    With burial amongst their auncestors.
    Here *Gothes* haue giuen me leaue to sheath my sword,
    Titus vnkinde, and careles of thine owne,
    Why sufferst thou thy sonnes vnburied yet,   90
    To houer on the dreadfull shore of stix,
    Make way to lay them by their brethren.
        They open the Tombe.
    There greete in silence as the dead are wont,
    And sleepe in peace, slaine in your Countries warres:
    O sacred Receptacle of my ioyes,
    Sweete Cell of vertue and Nobilitie,
    How many sonnes hast thou of mine in store,
    That thou wilt neuer render to me more.
        Sound Trumpets, and lay the Coffin in the Tombe.
    In peace and honour rest you here my sonnes,
    Roomes readiest Champions, repose you here in rest,   100
    Secure from worldly chaunces and mishaps:
    Here lurks no treason, here no enuie swels,
    Here grow no damned drugges, here are no stormes,
    No noyse, but silence and eternall sleepe,
    In peace and honour rest you here my sonnes.
        Enter Lauinia.
[*Lauinia.*] In peace and honour, liue Lord *Titus* long,
    My Noble Lord and father liue in fame:
    Lo at this Tombe my tributarie teares,
    I render for my brethrens obsequies:
    And at thy feete I kneele, with teares of ioy   110
    Shed on this earth, for thy returne to Rome,
    O blesse me here with thy victorious hand,
    Whose fortunes Roomes best Citizens applaud.

Titus. Kinde Rome that hast louingly reserude,
 The Cordiall of mine age to glad my hart,
 Lauinia liue, outliue thy fathers daies,
 And fames eternall date for vertues praise.
Marcus. Long liue Lord *Titus* my beloued brother,
 Gratious triumpher in the eies of Rome.
Titus. Thanks gentle Tribune, Noble brother *Marcus.*   120
Marcus. And welcome Nephews from succesfull wars
 You that suruiue, and you that sleepe in fame:
 Faire Lords, your fortunes are alike in all,
 That in your Countries seruice drew your swords,
 But safer triumph is this funerall pompe,
 That hath aspirde to Solons happines,
 And triumphs ouer chaunce in honours bed.
 Titus Andronicus, the people of Rome,
 Whose friend in iustice thou hast euer beene,
 Send thee by mee their Tribune and their trust,   130
 This Palliament of white and spotles hue,
 And name thee in election for the Empire,
 With these our late deceased Emperours sonnes:
 Be *Candidatus* then and put it on,
 And helpe to set a head on headles Roome.
Titus. A better head her glorious bodie fits,
 Than his that shakes for age and feeblenes:
 What should I don this Roabe and trouble you?
 Be chosen with Proclamations to daie,
 To morrow yeeld vp rule, resigne my life,
 And set abroad new busines for you all.
 Roome I haue beene thy souldier fortie yeares,
 And led my Countries strength succesfullie,
 And buried one and twentie valiant sonnes
 Knighted in Field, slaine manfullie in Armes,
 In right and seruice of their Noble Countrie:
 Giue me a staffe of Honour for mine age,
 But not a scepter to controwle the world,
 Vpright he held it Lords that held it last.
Marcus. *Titus* thou shalt obtaine & aske the Emperie.   150
Saturni⟨nus⟩. Proud and ambitious Tribune canst thou tell.
Titus. Patience Prince *Saturninus*.
Saturninus. Romaines doe me right.
 Patricians draw your swords and sheath them not,
 Till *Saturninus* be Romes Emperour:
 Andronicus would thou were shipt to hell,
 Rather than robbe me of the peoples harts.

Lucius. Prowd *Saturnine*, interrupter of the good,
    That noble minded *Titus* meanes to thee.
Titus. Content thee Prince, I will restore to thee   160
    The peoples harts, and weane them from themselues.
Bassianus. Andronicus I doo not flatter thee,
    But honour thee and will doo till I die:
    My faction if thou strengthen with thy friends
    I will most thankefull be, and thanks to men
    Of Noble minds, is honourable meede.
Titus. People of Rome, and peoples Tribunes here,
    I aske your voyces and your suffrages,
    Will yee bestow them friendly on *Andronicus.*
Tribunes. To gratifie the good *Andronicus*,   170
    And gratulate his safe returne to Rome,
    The people will accept whom he admits.
Titus. Tribunes I thanke you, and this sute I make,
    That you create our Emperours eldest sonne,
    Lord *Saturnine*: whose vertues will I hope,
    Reflect on Rome as [Tytans] Raies on earth,
    And ripen iustice in this Common weale:
    Then if you will elect by my aduise,
    Crowne him and say, *Long liue our Emperour.*
Marcus An⟨dronicus⟩. With voyces and applause of euery sort,   180
    Patricians and *Plebeans*, we create
    Lord *Saturninus* Romes great Emperour,
    And say *Long liue our Emperour* Saturnine,
        [*Marcus and the other Tribunes, with Saturninus and Bassianus,*
        come downe.]
Saturnine. Titus Andronicus, for thy fauours done,
    To vs in our election this day,
    I giue thee thankes in part of thy deserts,
    And will with deeds requite thy gentlenes:
    And for an onset *Titus* to aduance,
    Thy name and honourable familie,
    Lauinia will I make my Empresse,   190
    Romes Royall Mistris, Mistris of my hart,
    And in the sacred [Pāthean] her espouse:
    Tell me *Andronicus* doth this motion please thee.
Titus. It doth my worthie Lord, and in this match,
    I hold me highly Honoured of your Grace,
    And here in sight of Rome to *Saturnine*,
    King and Commander of our common weale,
    The wide worlds Emperour, doe I consecrate
    My sword, my Chariot, and my Prisoners,

Presents well worthy Romes imperious Lord: 200
Receiue them then, the tribute that I owe,
Mine honours Ensignes humbled at thy feete.
Saturnine. Thankes Noble *Titus* Father of my life,
How proude I am of thee and of thy gifts
Rome shall record, and when I doe forget
The least of these vnspeakeable deserts,
Romans forget your Fealtie to me.
Titus. Now Madam are you prisoner to an Emperour.
To him that for your honour and your state,
Will vse you Nobly, and your followers.   210
Saturnine. A goodly Lady trust me of the hue,
That I would choose were I to choose a new:
Cleare vp faire Queene that cloudy countenance,
Though [chance] of war hath wrought this change of chear
Thou comst not to be made a scorne in Rome.
Princely shall be thy vsage euerie waie.
Rest on my word, and let not discontent,
Daunt all your hopes, Madam he comforts you,
Can make you greater than the Queene of *Gothes*.
Lauinia you are not displeasde with this.   220
Lauinia. Not I my Lord, sith true Nobilitie,
Warrants these words in Princely curtesie.
Saturnine. Thanks sweete *Lauinia*, Romans let vs goe,
Raunsomles here we set our prisoners free,
Proclaime our Honours Lords with Trumpe and Drum.
[*Exeunt Saturninus, Tamora, Demetrius, Chiron, and Aron the Moore.*]
Bassianus. Lord *Titus* by your leaue, this maid is mine.
Titus. How sir, are you in earnest then my Lord?
Bascianus. I Noble *Titus* and resolude withall,
To doo my selfe this reason and this right.
Marcus. Suum [*cuique*] is our Romane iustice,   230
This Prince in iustice ceazeth but his owne.
Lucius. And that he will, and shall if *Lucius* liue.
Titus. Traitors auaunt, where is the Emperours gard?
      Enter aloft the Emperour with Tamora and her two sonnes
      and Aron the moore.
Treason my Lord, *Lauinia* is surprizde.
Saturnine. Surprizde, by whom?
Bascianus. By him that iustly may,
Beare his betrothde from all the world away.
     [*Exeunt Bassianus, Marcus, Lauinia, and the sonnes of Titus.*]
Titus. Follow my Lord, and Ile soone bring her backe.

Emperour. No *Titus*, no, the Emperour needes her not,
    Nor her, nor thee, nor any of thy stocke: 240
    Ile trust by leysure, him that mocks me once,
    Thee neuer, nor thy traiterous hawtie sonnes,
    Confederates all thus to dishonour mee.
    Was none in Rome to make a stale
    But *Saturnine*? Full well *Andronicus*
    Agree these deeds, with that prowd bragge of thine,
    That saidst I begd the Empire at thy hands.
Titus. O monstrous, what reprochfull words are these?
Saturn⟨inus⟩. But goe thy waies, goe giue that changing piece,
    To him that florisht for her with his sword: 250
    A valiant sonne in law thou shalt inioy,
    One fit to bandie with thy lawlesse sonnes,
    To ruffle in the Common-wealth of Rome.
Titus. These words are rasors to my wounded hart.
Satur⟨ninus⟩. And therfore louely *Tamora* Queene of Gothes,
    That like the statelie [*Phebe*] mongst her Nymphs,
    Dost ouershine the gallanst Dames of Rome,
    If thou be pleasde with this my sodaine choise,
    Behold I choose thee *Tamora* for my Bride,
    And will create thee Empresse of Rome.   260
    Speake Queene of Gothes dost thou applaud my choise?
    And here I sweare by all the Romane Gods,
    Sith Priest and holy water are so neere,
    And tapers burne so bright, and euery thing
    In readines for *Hymeneus* stand,
    I will not resalute the streets of Rome,
    Or clime my Pallace, till from forth this place,
    I lead espowsde my Bride along with mee.
Tamora. And here in sight of heauen to Rome I sweare,
    If *Saturnine* aduaunce the Queene of Gothes,   270
    Shee will a handmaide be to his desires,
    A louing Nurse, a Mother to his youth.
Sat⟨urninus⟩. Ascend faire Queene Panthean: Lords accompany
    Your Noble Emperour and his louelie Bride,
    Sent by the Heauens for Prince *Saturnine*,
    Whose wisdome hath her Fortune conquered,
    There shall wee consummate our spousall rites.
                             Exeunt Omnes.
Titus. I am not bid to wait vpon this bride,
    Titus when wert thou wont to walke alone,
    Dishonoured thus and challenged of wrongs.   280

Enter Marcus and Titus sonnes.

Marcus. My Lord to step out of these dririe dumps,
 How comes it that the subtile Queene of *Gothes*,
 Is of a sodaine thus aduaunc'd in Rome.
Titus. I know not *Marcus*, but I know it is.
 (Whether by deuise or no, the heauens can tell.)
 Is shee not then beholding to the man,
 That brought her for this high good turne so farre.
[*Marcus.* Yes, and will Nobly him remunerate.]

  Enter the Emperour, Tamora ⎫ ⎧ *Enter at the other doore*
  and her two sonnes, with ⎬ ⎨ *Bascianus and Lauinia,*
  the Moore at one doore. ⎭ ⎩ *with others.*

Saturnine. So *Bascianus*, you haue plaid your prize,
 God giue you ioy sir of your gallant Bride.   290
Bascianus. And you of yours my Lord, I say no more,
 Nor wish no lesse, and so I take my leaue.
Saturnine. Traitor, if Rome haue law, or we haue power,
 Thou and thy faction shall repent this Rape.
Bassianus. Rape call you it my Lord to ceaze my owne,
 My true betrothed loue, and now my wife:
 But let the lawes of Rome determine all,
 Meane while am I possest of that is mine.
Saturnine. Tis good sir, you are verie short with vs,
 But if we liue, weele be as sharpe with you.   300
Bascianus. My Lord what I haue done as best I may,
 Answere I must, and shall doo with my life,
 Onely thus much I giue your Grace to know,
 By all the dueties that I owe to Rome,
 This Noble Gentleman Lord *Titus* here,
 Is in opinion and in honour wrongd,
 That in the rescue of *Lauinia*,
 [   ]
 In zeale to you, and highly moude to wrath,
 To be controwld in that he frankelie gaue,   310
 Receaue him then to fauour *Saturnine*,
 That hath exprest himselfe in all his deeds,
 A father and a friend to thee and Rome.
Titus. Prince *Bascianus* leaue to pleade my deeds, ·
 Tis thou, and those, that haue dishonoured me,
 Rome and the righteous heauens be my iudge,
 How I haue loude and honoured *Saturnine*.
Tamora. My worthy Lord, if euer *Tamora*,
 Were gratious in those Princelie eies of thine,

Then heare me speake indifferently for all: 320
  And at my sute (sweete) pardon what is past.
Saturnine. What Madam be dishonoured openly,
  And baselie put it vp without reuenge.
Tamora. Not so my Lord, the Gods of Rome forfend
  I should be Authour to dishonour you.
  But on mine honour dare I vndertake,
  For good Lord *Titus* innocence in all,
  Whose furie not dissembled speakes his griefes:
  Then at my sute looke gratiouslie on him,
  Loose not so noble a friend on vaine suppose,   330
  Nor with sowre looks afflict his gentle hart.
  My Lord: Be rulde by me, be wonne at last,
  Dissemble all your griefes and discontents,
  You are but newlie planted in your Throne,
  Least then the people, and Patricians too,
  Vpon a iust suruay take Titus part,
  And so supplant you for ingratitude,
  Which Rome reputes to be a hainous sinne,
  Yeeld at intreats: and then let me alone,
  Ile find a day to massacre them all,   340
  And race their faction and their familie,
  The cruell father, and his traiterous sonnes,
  To whom I sued for my deare sonnes life.
  And make them know what tis to let a Queene,
  Kneele in the streets and begge for grace in vaine.
  Come, come sweete Emperour, (come *Andronicus*:)
  Take vp this good old man, and cheare the hart,
  That dies in tempest of thy angrie frowne.
Saturnine. Rise *Titus* rise, my Empresse hath preuaild.
Titus. I thanke your Maiestie, and her my Lord,   350
  These words, these looks, infuse new life in me.
Tamora. *Titus* I am incorporate in Rome,
  A Roman now adopted happilie,
  And must aduise the Emperour for his good,
  This day all quarrels die *Andronicus*.
  And let it be mine honour good my Lord,
  That I haue reconciled your friends and you.
  For you Prince *Bassianus* I haue past
  My word and promise to the Emperour,
  That you will be more milde and tractable.   360
  And feare not Lords, and you *Lauinia*,
  By my aduise all humbled on your knees,
  You shall aske pardon of his Maiestie.

[*Lucius.*] Wee doo, and vowe to Heauen and to his Highnes,
　　That what wee did, was mildlie as we might,
　　Tendring our sisters honour and our owne.
Marcus. That on mine honour here doo I protest.
Saturnine. Away, and talke not, trouble vs no more.
Tamora. Nay, nay sweet Emperor, we must all be friends,
　　The Tribune and his Nephews kneele for grace,　　　　　　　370
　　I will not be denied, sweete hart looke backe.
Saturnine. Marcus, for thy sake, and thy brothers here,
　　And at my louelie *Tamoras* intreats,
　　I doo remit these young mens hainous faults,
　　Stand vp: *Lauinia* though you left me like a Churle,
　　I found a friend, and sure as death I swore,
　　I would not part a Batchiler from the Priest.
　　Come if the Emperours Court can feast two Brides,
　　You are my guest *Lauinia* and your friends:
　　This daie shall be a loue-daie *Tamora*.　　　　　　　　　380
Titus. To morrow and it please your Maiestie,
　　To hunt the Panther and the Hart with me,
　　With horne and hound, weele giue your grace boniour.
Saturnine. Be it so *Titus* and gramercie too.　　　　　*Exeunt.*
　　　　　sound trumpets, manet Moore.
Aron. Now climeth *Tamora* Olympus toppe,

Substantive Emendations
　36　y^e] E. K. CHAMBERS; that Q1
　176　Tytans] Q2; Tytus Q1
　192　Pāthean] F2; Pathan Q1
　214　chance] Q2; change Q1
　230　*cuique*] F2; *cuiqum* Q1
　256　Phebe] F2; *Thebe* Q1
　273　Queene Panthean:] POPE (*subs.*); ~: ~ˌ Q1
　288] *from* F1; *not in* Q1
　364　*Lucius.*] ROWE (*after* F1); *not in* Q1. *Lucius normally acts as*
　　　spokesman, but more than one son may speak.

Incidental Emendations (Q1's reading is to the right of the bracket)
　　8　indignitie.] ~,
　14　vertue consecrate,] ~, ~ˌ
　59　right,] ~.
　216　waie.] ~ˌ
　230　iustice] iustce

248 *Titus.*] ~ₐ
310 gaue,] ~.
324 forfendₐ] ~.
338 sinne,] ~.
349 preuaild.] ~,
365 mildlie] mildₐie

INDEX